James Egan was born in in 1985 and lived in Portarlington, Co. Laois in the Midlands of Ireland for most of his life. In 2008, James moved to England and studied in Oxford. James married his wife in 2012 and currently lives in Havant in Hampshire. James was a volunteer for the Halow charity for disabled young people in Guildford. James had his first book, 365 Ways to Stop Sabotaging Your Life published in 2014.

<u>Books by James Egan</u>

100 Classic Stories in 100 Pages
1000 Facts about Comic Book Characters
500 Facts About Godzilla
365 Ways to Stop Sabotaging Your Life

365 Things People Believe That Aren't True
365 More Things People Believe That Aren't True
Another 365 Things People Believe That Aren't
True

Or get the three books in one as
1000 Things People Believe That Aren't True

<u>Fiction</u>
Fairytale
Inherit the Earth

500 Things People Believe That Aren't True

By
JAMES EGAN

Dedicated

To

Laura

Introduction

At the end of 2014, I published 365 Things People Believe That Aren't True. One of the facts in that book was how the brontosaurus was not a real dinosaur. Archeologists have accepted this fact for over a century.

Earlier this year, experts have reclassified the brontosaurus as a dinosaur.
As a result, I had to remove that fact from my old book. I wasn't wrong. I was just correct at the time. But circumstances out of my control made that fact no longer valid.

I never intended to write another book but I was under the false pretense that I covered every misconception. But that's impossible as facts change daily. Pluto used to be a planet. Thomas Edison was considered a great inventor but now he is seen as a charlatan.

I assumed I would struggle to find another 365 misconceptions to cover another book.
On the contrary, misinformation spreads so quickly nowadays thanks to the Internet, I was able to find 500 new misconceptions.

If you know of any other misconceptions, please let me know on Twitter under my username @jameswzegan85.

Content

ANIMALS

1. **You should feed fish to a cat.**
   Cats are allergic to fish. Never feed them, no matter how much they beg... even if they look really cute.

2. **Mice eat cheese.**
   Mice don't even like cheese.

3. **All vultures eat meat.**
   The palm-nut vulture is a vegetarian.

4. **Boa constrictors are dangerous.**
   When people think of a constrictor (a snake that wraps itself around its prey,) boas come to mind. However, boas have never caused a single human death. Only pythons have.

5. **Flies live only for a few hours.**
   Flies live for a month.
      Mayflies are also accused of living for a day (their Latin name means "short-lived.") A mayfly has four stages of life (the final stage being at least a day.) But its overall life can be up to four years.

6. **Bulls are enraged upon seeing the color red.**
   Bulls are color blind. When matadors wave their red cape to a bull, the bull becomes angry because it doesn't like anything being waved in front of it.

7. **The average person eats eight spiders a year.**
Arachnophobes rejoice! This silly Internet rumor
is nonsense. (But your phobia is a bit silly.)

8. **All spiders weave webs.**
Only half of them do. And if you don't find that fact
particularly interesting, it's not uncommon for
spiders to get trapped in their own web. Basically,
spiders are the Wile E. Coyote of the animal
kingdom.

9. **Bats are blind.**
Bats have terrible eyesight and rely on
echolocation but none of the 1,015 species of bats
are blind.

10. **All ducks quack.**
Only the female ducks can quack. There are some
species of duck that can't quack at all and instead
grunt or whistle.

11. **Crabs have eight legs.**
Crabs have ten legs. Their two front claws are
also used to help them move around.

12. **Koala bears are bears.**
They are marsupials and are more related to the
wombat than the bear.

13. **Elephants are scared of mice.**
This has become popularized from Looney Tunes
cartoons but it's untrue.

14.   A cheetah is fast enough to catch any prey.
It's common knowledge that cheetahs are the fastest land animals. They can go from zero to sixty miles per hour in three seconds. Although they have a maximum speed of seventy-five miles per hour, they can't maintain it for very long. If they haven't caught their prey within seconds of reaching this speed, they will stop due to exhaustion.

15.   Lobsters scream when they are boiled.
The "screaming" sound is steam escaping from the lobsters' shells.

16.   Snails have shells and slugs don't.
To comprehend the subtle differences between the two, you would need a comprehensive biological understanding of gastropods. (It would take at least ten pages to explain and would require me to use words like "Basommathophora" and "Papillodermatoidea." Spellcheck doesn't even accept these terms as words on my Mac.

Long story short, some slugs sport a shell and some snails bear no shell. The shell is not a defining characteristic of either creature.

17.   Komodo dragons have a powerful bite.
Despite the fact that this ten-foot reptile is the world's largest lizard, its bite is weaker than a cat's. However, the venom in its mouth is so venomous, it doesn't need a strong bite to kill its prey.

18.   Sharks have bad eyesight.
A shark's eyesight is so good that it can see an
object at night ten times clearer than we can see
at daytime. Oh, sharks. Is there anything they
can't do?

19.   Sharks are dangerous.
Of the four hundred species of shark, only twelve
of them are dangerous to humans. Nevertheless,
shark attacks are extremely rare.

20.   Sharks eat anything.
Sharks are quite particular about what they eat.
They don't like eating creatures with a lot of
bones (including us) because they are difficult to
digest. Most sharks only eat very specific fish and
the whale shark only eats plankton.

21.   Sharks have huge, sharp teeth.
Only some sharks have sharp teeth but almost all
sharks have tiny teeth. The great white shark's
teeth are razor sharp but they are very small.

**22.   If a shark was about to attack you, you should
punch it in the nose.**
Humans don't have the strength to punch
anything underwater. Next time you are in the
swimming pool, try punching someone
underwater (with their permission of course.)
If you are about to be attacked by a
carnivorous shark, you should poke its eyes or
grabs its gills.

23. **Sharks have no predators.**
Killer whales (which are actually dolphins) kill sharks.

24. **Anteaters are harmless.**
You'd think a slow, nearly deaf, almost blind, toothless animal who only eats ants would be harmless to humans, wouldn't you? However, they have been known to kill humans with their huge claws. If you see an anteater, stay away.

25. **Kangaroos are harmless.**
Despite the fact that kangaroos are really cute, they can be dangerous to humans. Their springy legs are so powerful, they can easily shatter your bones with one swift kick. They are also really good boxers. Seriously. They will box rival kangaroos to death.

26. **A goldfish only grows to the size of its bowl.**
There's no science to back this up.

27. **Hippos eat humans.**
Although hippos kill about five thousand people per year, hippos are vegetarians. They only attack humans when they enter a hippo's domain.

28. **Hippos can swim.**
In spite of the amount of time they spend underwater, hippos can't swim. They can hold their breath longer than any other land mammal (about twenty minutes) so they don't need to learn to swim to survive.

29.   You can't teach an old dog new tricks.
This is just an expression that some people take seriously.

30.   If bees went extinct, humans would die out.
The extinction of all beekind would greatly affect mankind and the world in general but we are adaptable enough to survive.

Bees pollinate plant life. The cycle of bees pollinating flowers is responsible for 70% of all fruit, vegetables, nuts, and seeds. Not only would this drastically affect our food consumption but these foods are responsible for $200 billion worth of agricultural revenue which would collapse countless corporations and cause millions of people to lose their jobs. So the bee's extinction would devastate human life, but it wouldn't end it.

31.   Zebras have stripes for camouflage.
Unless the grass is black and white, zebras aren't going to hide from predators.

Flies are attracted to black surfaces so they tend to chill out on black animals. A zebra's black stripes protect them from the sun but the white stripes confuse the flies so insects don't often land on them.

32.   A lone wolf would attack a human.
Wolves are pack animals. If a pack animal were to see a human, it would run away.

33. **The biggest land animal in Antarctica is the polar bear.**

Polar bears don't live in Antarctica.

If you were smart enough to know that, you would probably guess the answer is the penguin.

But that's wrong too. Penguins spend almost all of their time under water so are not classified as land animals.

If you are exceptionally sneaky, you may imagine the answer to be a human. But humans aren't native in Antarctica nor could they sustain life there for very long.

The largest land animal in Antarctica is the teeny-weeny midge insect.

34. **Penguins can only live in the cold.**

The Galapagos penguin is the only penguin that lives in the tropics.

35. **Rats are a minor nuisance.**

In rural or poor regions, rats destroy or contaminate up to 40% of ALL food. They can eat up to 20% of crops and then eat another 20% of grain in storage. Throughout the world, rats are thought to eat or destroy up to 10% of all food humans produce.

<u>BOOKS</u>

36.   In Romeo and Juliet, Juliet's line, "Romeo, Romeo, wherefore art thou, Romeo?" means "where are you, Romeo?"

        Hundreds of Shakespeare lines are misunderstood but this is the most famous example. This line means, "Why are you Romeo?" This is in reference to how she loves Romeo but his family is in conflict with her family. So she's basically asking, "Why did I have to fall in love with Romeo even though our families hate each other?"

        That's all from one line. Shakespeare is REALLY hard.

37.   In Shawshank Redemption, Red (Morgan Freeman's character) is black.

        Red is a white Irishman in the short story, Shawshank Redemption. When the main character asks him why he is called Red, he says, "Because I'm Irish." This line was kept in the movie as a joke. Because Morgan Freeman is not Irish. Just in case you couldn't tell.

38.   Gulliver's Travels ends with Gulliver reuniting with his family.

        Gulliver goes mad from all of his adventures and abandons his family to live in a stable. The book concludes with him deranged, desperately trying to talk to a horse… Why did he go on his journeys again?

39. **The Wooden Horse of Troy is first mentioned in Homer's epic, The Iliad.**

The Iliad concludes before the Wooden Horse invades Troy. The Wooden Horse is discussed in hindsight in the sequel, The Odyssey. It is elaborated on in more depth in the following book, The Aeneid.

40. **Waiting for Godot is about God.**

Samuel Beckett wrote this play in French while he was living in France for years. "God" is "dieu" in French and he never thought the name "Godot" would be mistaken for "God."

41. **In Lord of the Rings, Gandalf leaves Bilbo's ring with Frodo for several months before he learns that it is the One Ring.**

If you remember the movie, Gandalf is suspicious of Bilbo's ring so he leaves to research it. He returns several months later to inform Frodo that it is the One Ring.

In the book however, Gandalf doesn't leave for several months. He leaves for seventeen years! They had to shorten this for the film because... come on... it was already way too long.

42. **In 20,000 Leagues Under the Sea, the ship plunges 20,000 leagues.**

20,000 leagues is six times wider than the diameter of Earth. The deepest anyone travels in this book is ten miles. Ten Miles Under the Sea didn't exactly have a good ring to it though. The ship travels 20,000 leagues in distance, not depth.

**43.   In 20,000 Leagues Under the Sea, the crew
battle with Giant Squids.**

> They battle with giant octopi (which are not a
> real animal.) Now you might think – Squid?
> Octopus? Who cares?
>
> > I do. I care.

**44.   F. Scott Fitzgerald wrote many great novels,
especially The Great Gatsby.**

> F. Scott heavily based characters off his wife,
> Zelda in his stories. That may not sound like a big
> deal. Authors based characters on real people all
> of the time. However, F. Scott didn't just
> incorporate Zelda's private life into his stories. He
> took lines from her love letters and diaries word-
> for-word and put them in his novels without
> telling her.
>
> I am not saying that she should get the credit
> instead but her biographer, Kendall Taylor has
> reviewed all of F. Scott's work and concluded that
> so much of it stems from Zelda that she should at
> least be considered a co-author.

**45.   Cinderella's glass slipper is a mistranslation.
The slipper is actually made of squirrel fur.**

> There has been a theory circulating the Internet
> that Cinderella's "glass" slipper is a mistranslation
> of the word "squirrel." This theory sounds
> plausible since Cinderella was written in French
> where fur (vair) and glass (verre) sound similar.
> However, Perrault's version isn't the original
> Cinderella story. It is simply the most famous. But
> in every version, the slipper is glass.

46.   Comic books are all about superheroes.

Believing that all comic books are about superheroes is like saying that all movies are about Transformers. Transformers is well known because it is a billion-dollar franchise but there are countless other films. Action films always makes the most money but that doesn't change the fact that there are many other genres of film.

Comics are exactly the same. Superhero comics are by far the most successful, especially nowadays thanks to the success of comic book movies but there are thousands of comics about romance, noir, crime, comedy, horror, etc.

47.   Catcher in the Rye concludes with the main character ending up in a mental institution.

The story ends with the lead character dying in a tuberculosis ward.

48.   Writers can't maintain an income if they self-publish their books.

Virginia Woolf, Mark Twain, Beatrix Potter, D. H. Laurence, James Joyce, and Alexander Pope self-published their books and created incredible works like Peter Rabbit, Ulysses, and Huckleberry Finn.

Even the poet, William Blake, made his own ink, hand printed his own pages, and got his wife to sew on the covers.

Thanks to eBooks, self-publishing books is easier than ever and it's easier to maintain an income.

DINOSAURS

49.   Pterodactyls were dinosaurs.
"Pterodactyl" is a word people use when they mean "flying dinosaur" but experts never used this term. When you think of the word "pterodactyl," the image you get in your mind is that of a pteradon.

50.   Okay, so pteradons were dinosaurs.
Dinosaurs couldn't fly. There's this other misconception that pteradons were birds. All flying lizards (known as pterosaurs) during this era were reptiles but they weren't dinosaurs.

51.   Dinosaurs had two brains.
Some dinosaurs like the Brachiosaurus were so immense, that it was theorized that they couldn't have one brain transmitting signals and impulses as they would take too long to travel through the body. It was believed that they might have a second brain in their gut. This theory has never been taken seriously nor has there ever been any evidence to suggest it's true. Nevertheless, some people believe it. It was even referenced in the movie Pacific Rim. For some reason.

52.   The T-Rex had small arms.
The T-Rex's three-foot arms seem small compared to its eighteen-foot body but they were strong enough to lift 430lbs. Each. The maximum

a human could bicep curl with one hand is 260lbs. Get that T-Rex a gym membership.

53. **Dinosaurs were lizards.**
Dinosaurs were their own category of reptile.

54. **There are complete T-Rex fossils in museums.**
Despite the fact that they are the most famous dinosaur ever, not a single complete T-Rex skeleton has every been found.

55. **"Dinosaur" means "terrible lizard."**
Richard Owen coined the term "dinosaur" in 1842. He said it meant "fearfully great lizard" but people simplified it over time.

56. **Dinosaurs were the first reptiles.**
Dinosaurs aren't as old as we originally thought. Archeologists used to believe that dinosaurs were 600-million-year-old but recent studies show that they are more like 231.4 million years old.

Reptiles emerged between 320-310 million years ago.

ENTERTAINMENT

57. **The audition in talent shows like Britain's Got Talent and American Idol is the first time the participants have performed for the talent show.**

In American Idol, the participants are accepted or rejected by two sets of producers before they perform to the main panel. That means they have gone through two auditions before they "surprise" the main panel.

Most talent shows follow similar strategies.

58. **The documentary, Super Size Me is accurate.**

In this 2004 documentary, Morgan Spurlock only eats McDonalds three times a day for thirty days. After he completed the challenge, he learned that his cholesterol levels became catastrophically high. During this extreme diet, he experienced depression, mood swings and liver damage. This is because he was eating 5,000 calories daily.

Or so he claimed. No study has been able to replicate Spurlock's results. Sweden's University of Linkoping did the same test on a bunch of students and none of them had the same results as Spurlock, nor were they able to consume 5,000 calories a day.

59. **The Disney film, Fantasia concludes with a scene with The Devil.**

The dark creature at the end of the movie is Czernobog, the Slavic Black God. Remember… this is a Disney movie. For children.

60.   Cool Runnings is a true story.
Although Jamaica did enter the Winter Olympics in 1988 as the movie states, the characters on the team are fictional.

The other teams didn't bully or antagonize Jamaica's team. They were very supportive to the Jamaican bobsledders, especially the Germans (who were evil in the movie because of course they were.)

In the movie, the team crashes in their final race. This happened in real life but they didn't hoist the sled above themselves. This was added for effect. In reality, they just carried it.

Nevertheless, Cool Runnings is still the greatest film ever made. Ever.

61.   The mafia inspired the mob in The Godfather.
The Godfather didn't copy the traits of the mafia. Ironically, it was the mafia that copied The Godfather! The mafia never even used the word "Godfather" before the film was released.

The movie defined the mob as men of honor who saw each other as a family rather than friends or business partners. They dressed well and had legitimate businesses. They were respected and feared even by the law. In Tim Adler's book, Hollywood and the Mob, he said that the mafia were "pig-ignorant, violent-sentimental goombahs" before The Godfather came out. The mafia wanted to be associated with their depiction in the movie which is often considered to be the greatest film ever made (after Cool Runnings, of course.)

62.   Citizen Kane won an Oscar for Best Picture.
Even if you have never seen Citizen Kane nor know what it is about, you should be aware that it is commonly considered to be one of, if not the greatest film ever made. (Juuuuust behind Cool Runnings.)

Nevertheless, it only won an Oscar for Best Screenplay in 1941. How Green Is My Valley won for Best Picture that year.

63.   Erin Brockovich won her clients millions of dollars as is shown in the movie of the same name.
The firm behind the movie, Erin Brockovich raked in millions of dollars from the settlement earmarked for cancer patients and made the townspeople wait six months before they received their settlement (although many people did not receive anything near the amount they were promised.)

<u>EXERCISE</u>

64. **If you stop exercising, your muscles turn to fat.**

Muscles can't change into fat. Fat and muscle are made up of two completely different chemical compounds. It's like saying a chair can turn into a donkey. Your muscles will shrink if you stop exercising and your fat may grow if you can't burn it off. One will not switch to the other.

65. **A muscular person is the epitome of fitness.**

Some of the most muscular people I have ever met have never been inside a gym. They may drink, smoke, eat bad food but they have the results most people dream of. Why?

Most muscular people can thank their genetics for their body rather than working out.

When you want to build your muscles, don't just copy what a muscular person says. What that person does may suit his or her genetics. You may hurt yourself. Do research, try different things and then learn what suits you.

66. **If you exercise before you go to bed, you won't be able to sleep.**

Yes you will. Because you will be exhausted. Researchers have stated that exercising in the morning is best but no evidence has been shown that working out in the evening will damage your sleep pattern.

67.   During your workout, the maximum your heart rate should be is 220 minus your age.

Let's say a 20-year-old follows this rule. That means a 20 year olds' heart rate should never be higher than 200 (because 220-20=200) to maximize how many calories he or she would burn.

What people need to grasp when it comes to exercise is there is no secret technique to get the results you desire quickly. You can't cheat your way to your goals because everyone's body is different. Some people work out better with a lower heart rate and some people work out better with a higher heart rate. You need to play around to see what way suits you.

68.   Diets work.

A day will never come where we find a Perfect Diet. Your body will adapt to any diet because evolution has made your body exceptionally good at storing fat. You can't trick it in the long run with fad diets.

Eat 2,000 calories a day. Have a balanced amount of carbs, fats, and proteins. Exercise. Get a good amount of sleep. That's it. That is the greatest way to stay in shape.

Diets are short-term solutions that your body will eventually get used to. Most diets will make you run the risk of injuring yourself or getting ill.

Instead of a diet, just make life choices. Decide what foods need to be in your daily routine and what foods you need to do without.

69. The more you sweat when you exercise, the more fat you lose.

Sweat and fat loss are not connected. If you sweat profusely when you exercise, you will become dehydrated. Make sure you drink plenty of water if you want to lose fat.

70. Muscular people are strong.

Big muscles don't mean strong muscles. Likewise, small muscles don't mean weak muscles.

Everyone knows someone who is quite small but has surprisingly stamina and strength.

One of my friends is incredibly muscular but he can't do two push-ups! A person can naturally have big muscles but that doesn't necessarily mean he or she will be strong.

71. Cardio burns more calories than weight training.

You may burn more calories in cardio than weight training but you continue to burn calories AFTER you finish weight training. This is called the AfterBurn Effect and has been popularized by Mike Chang who has become popular on Youtube thanks to his channel - SixPackShortCuts.

Mike says that the AfterBurn technique means you can burn calories forty-eight hours (if not longer) after you finish your exercise. This means that you can be sitting at work while your body is burning calories. If you want to desperately burn calories, go for weight training.

72. Calorie counters on exercise machines are accurate.

Some cardiovascular machines like treadmills will claim to count the calories you've burned. So if you ran on a treadmill for an hour, the machine may say that you have burned 200 calories.

But how does that work? Depending on your size, age, gender, and genetics, you could burn 2,000 calories per day or 5,000 calories per day. Calorie counters might give you an extra incentive to burn that last ten calories but it's not very accurate.

73. If you work on one muscle group, that group will grow faster.

When you do a bicep curl, you are not just working your bicep. You are working your triceps, your shoulders, your back, and your abs.

All of your muscles are connected and linked to one another. If you try to focus on certain muscles, you will still be using other muscles throughout your body. If you want a six-pack, you will get better results working on your abs, your chest, your shoulders, your arms, and your legs rather than working on just your abs every day.

74. Vitamin tablets work.

Water-soluble vitamins like B1, B2, B3, B6, B12, C, folic acid, biotin, and pantothenic acid can't be stored in your body's fat reserve for the same reason water and oil don't mix. Once you exceed the daily-required amount, they will be eliminated through your urine.

75.   You should rest if you pull a muscle.
Rest can be the worst thing you can possibly do if you injure a muscle. Each type of injury varies so it's best to ask a physiotherapist or doctor. For some muscle injuries, you need to rest as much as possible.

    For other muscle injuries, you will need to stay active to prevent the muscle from seizing up. In this state, your body will scream for you to relax but you can't. You obviously shouldn't do anything overly strenuous but don't rest for the whole day. A bit of walking every half an hour can make you heal much faster.

76.   Stretching prevents injury.
Thank God I was too impatient to ever stretch before exercising because it is proven to reduce stamina and strength by 2%. That's not a lot but it can make a difference in an important match or sports event.

    A quick warm-up is much more effective than static stretching.

77.   Running shoes should be replaced every six months.
This depends on too many factors to give an accurate answer. You need to factor in your height and weight, how you run, how often, time of year, etc. It's up to you when you feel your shoes are worn down. That could be three months or a year.

78. **Running on a treadmill will prevent knee injuries.**

People run differently on treadmills compared to running out in the open. This causes runners to have more bounce in their run. This impact can take its toll on your knees so it's not safer than running outside.

79. **Olympic athletes have a perfect diet to keep fit.**

At the 2012 Olympics, Usain Bolt ate a hundred chicken nuggets per day during his training.

Shot putter Dylan Armstrong needed up to 9,000 calories per day (an average is 2,000.)

Michael Phelps' swimming partner, Ryan Lochte, would eat almost 12,000 calories a day, mostly by consuming McDonalds'.

A lot of Olympic swimmers and runners will eat over 10,000 calories a day. They are not necessarily trying to eat healthy food. They just need as many calories as possible to burn off during their training.

FOOD AND DRINK

80.   A tomato is a fruit.
It's not. Accept it and move on with your life.

81.   Fine. A tomato is a vegetable.
It's not a vegetable either. A tomato is a weird little food. Botanists say that tomatoes are a fruit and a vegetable. No other food has this distinction.

82.   At fast-food restaurants, salads are the healthier choice.
Salads are covered in artificial sweeteners and loaded with sugar. In most restaurants, salads have more calories and more fat than a normal burger.

At a Wendy's restaurant, a Spicy Chicken Caesar Salad has more calories (780 calories) and more fat (51 grams) than a Pretzel Bacon Cheeseburger (680 calories and 36 grams of fat.)

So how do you avoid this dilemma? It's simple. Don't eat at a fast food restaurant.

83.   Microwaves cook food from the inside out.
It does the total opposite. Also, the more water the food has, the quicker it will heat.

84.   Espresso has more caffeine than coffee.
A cup of espresso has half the caffeine of a cup of coffee. Even the most powerful espresso will still be 20mg of caffeine short of the weakest coffee.

85. **Red Bull has more caffeine than coffee.**
Coca Cola has 23-25mgs of caffeine.
Red Bull has 75-80mgs of caffeine.
A cup of coffee has 95-200mgs of caffeine.

86. **You should drink caffeine in the morning to wake you up.**
Your body has an internal biological clock called the circadian rhythm that regulates many things about your body including how tired you feel. It controls your energy levels with a hormone called cortisol, which keeps you alert. Between 8-9am, your cortisol reaches its maximum level. If you interrupt the release of the hormone at this time with tea or coffee, the caffeine won't wake you up as much as it should. It will also make you build up a resistance to cortisol so you will have more reason to feel tired even if you consume caffeine regularly. It's best to consume caffeine after your cortisol peak at 10am.

87. **Caffeine increases the chances of osteoporosis.**
Caffeine degrades calcium in your bones but the difference is so negligible that you should be fine so long as you don't have sixteen cups a day.

88. **Caffeine helps you lose weight.**
One study looked at 58,000 people over twelve years and it revealed that the more caffeine people consumed, the more weight they put on. Also, how do you follow 58,000 people for twelve years without coming across as creepy?

89.   Caffeine increases the risk of heart disease.
At this point, I probably sound pretty defensive about caffeine. Nevertheless, there is no evidence to suggest moderate caffeine intake can cause damage to your heart.

90.   Caffeine is very dangerous.
It may appear that some coffee company is paying me to promote caffeine but I assure you that caffeine is very healthy in small doses. According to the Mayo clinic, it helps defend the body against Parkinson's, depression, type 2 diabetes, liver disease and liver cancer.

91.   Vodka is made from potatoes.
99% of all vodka worldwide is distilled from grain like wheat, rye, or corn.
There is even a vodka made from cow's milk called Pure Milk Vodka!
Trust me. I'm Irish.

92.   Mongolian BBQ is Mongolian.
It's Taiwanese.

93.   Italian dressing is Italian.
Italian dressing is American. American dressing didn't sound exotic enough so they renamed it.

94.   Spaghetti and meatballs is an Italian dish.
In my first book, I mention that spaghetti originates from China. You would assume that spaghetti and meatballs combo must be Italian. Nope! This is once again credited to America.

95. **Garlic bread is Italian.**
This is another American dish that the Italians unfairly get the credit for.

96. **Fajitas are Mexican.**
Once again, America gets the credit. Fajitas originate from Texas. I can't thank Texans enough for this.

97. **Chimichangas are from Mexico.**
They come from Arizona. What's with Italy and Mexico getting the credit for America's food?

98. **Apple pie is American.**
The one food you'd swear is American originated in England in 1381.

99. **The Coney dog comes from Coney Island.**
Three different restaurants claim to have invented the Coney dog but all three of these restaurants are in Michigan.

100. **Maraschino cherries are Italian.**
They're from the not-as-exotic land of Oregon, USA.

101. **French dip is French.**
French dip was invented in LA in 1918. Why do we even name things anymore??

102. **Tempura is Japanese.**
Tempura was made in Portugal 700 years ago.

103. Sauerkraut is German.
Even though the name of this sour cabbage sounds German, it has been available in China for two millennia.

104. German chocolate cake is German.
Sam German from Dallas concocted this American cake.

105. Baked Alaska dessert is from Alaska.
It's from New York.

106. You should wash chicken before cooking it.
Cooking a chicken will kill any potential bacteria. Washing it prior to cooking is redundant.

107. You can't smoke alcohol.
The idea behind alcohol smoking is to feel drunk without consuming calories.

This sounds too good to be true but alcohol smoking is possible. However, it is unreliable because it is impossible to tell how much alcohol is going into your system so it's more likely you could suffer alcohol poisoning.

108. Dark beer is bad for you.
Dark beer is only bad for you in excess (but that applies to anything.) Dark beer is full of fiber, iron, silicon, flavonoids, antioxidants, which can be good for the heart, osteoporosis and preventing blood clots.

109. Light beer will help you lose weight.
The difference between the "healthy" versions of
beer is insignificantly small. A Guinness Draught
has 125 calories. A light Guinness has 110
calories. Fifteen calories is almost nothing.

Also, people tend to drink more of the
"healthy" version of beer (or anything for that
matter) so having eight pints of light beer instead
of five pints of normal beer is going to help you
gain weight, not lose it.

110. Drinking with a meal will stop a hangover.
This works but only with red meat like a burger
or steak. Red meat has a high concentration of
amino acids and B vitamins, which will soak up
some of the alcohol and limit the risk of a
hangover.

111. Foods cooked with alcohol are non-alcoholic.
Some of the alcohol will evaporate as the food is
being cooked but up to 85% of the alcohol can
stay depending on how you cook your meal.

112. There is no beer in non-alcoholic beer.
There is 0.5% alcohol in an ordinary bottle of
non-alcoholic beer. It's false advertising but 0.5%
Beer doesn't have the same ring to it.

**113. You can get drunk from non-alcoholic beer if
you drink enough of it.**
You might feel a little bit tipsy if you drank thirty-
six of them in a row.

114. **"Beer before liquor, never been sicker, liquor before beer, you're in the clear."**
This archaic idea doesn't hold up. It's irrelevant how you drink your alcohol. The more you drink, the worse your hangover will be.

115. **There is no real cure for a hangover.**
You might think that there is no true cure for a hangover. But there is one simple technique that is surprisingly effective.

Bacon. Bacon has enough protein and fat to break down the amino acids necessary to boost your metabolism to help eradicate the hangover rapidly. Bacon. It solves everything.

116. **Agave nectar is better for you than sugar.**
Agave nectar has more fructose than any other sweetener (including high fructose corn syrup.) Too much fructose is extremely dangerous in the long run and can cause terminal pancreatitis.

Honey has 40% fructose.

White sugar has 50%.

Corn syrup has 55%.

Agave has at least 55% but it can be as high as 97%! There is also an extra third of calories in a tablespoon of agave compared to sugar.

117. **If a food is "local," it means that it's "organic."**
The FDA doesn't regulate the word "local" so there is no telling whether the food came from your local town or China or Mars. It's just a word suppliers slap onto their food to make it sound more healthy.

118. Organic food has more nutrients.

In 2014, research published in the British Journal of Nutrition looked at 343 studies of organic and non-organic food and found most vegetables had pretty much the same levels of the most significant nutrients (Vitamin C and E) whether they were organic or not.

These studies did confirm, however that organic food did have more antioxidants than non-organic. This shows that organic is healthier than non-organic but perhaps not as much as you would've imagined.

119. Natural food is healthy.

The U.S. Food and Drug Administration give a lot of wiggle room for what "natural food" means.

Even if a food has artificial flavors, added color, or synthetic substances, the FDA would still consider the food to be natural.

120. Brown sugar is healthier than white sugar.

Brown sugar IS white sugar except the molasses dye is removed from its coloring. This dye gives it a bit more calcium and potassium but not enough to make any significant difference to your body. They also have the same amount of calories.

121. Adding salt to boiling water cooks food faster.

To noticeably speed up how fast the food cooks, you would need to put in so much salt, it would render the food inedible.

122. **White chocolate is chocolate.**
White chocolate is composed of milk, vanilla, sugar, lecithin, cocoa butter, but above all, no chocolate.

123. **Brown eggs are healthier than white eggs.**
Egg color has nothing to do with the nutrition of the egg. The color has to do with the genetics of the hen that laid it.

124. **Vitamin Water is healthy.**
Vitamin water has so much sugar, it's basically Coke. No consumer should reasonably be misled into thinking that Vitamin Water is healthy.

125. **Margarine is healthier than butter.**
Margarine is considered to be healthier than butter because it lowers cholesterol. But that tends to only apply to tubs of margarine.

Stick margarine has trans-fat, which can lower HDL, also known as good cholesterol. That's right, not all cholesterol is bad.

126. **Genetic food is a recent concept.**
GMO's (genetically modified organisms) have been around since 12,000 BC. This was done with basic selective breeding and the domestication of plants and animals. By cultivating organisms with certain desired traits, generations of farmers have been able to selectively breed superior products for millennia.

127. **The sugar you eat is natural.**
     90% of the sugar in America (and most
     countries) comes from sugar beets with GMO's.

128. **Potatoes are a natural food.**
     Most potatoes worldwide are genetically
     modified to decrease the amount of acrylamide (a
     cancer-causing chemical.) This GM will make the
     potatoes resistant to bruising so they will last
     longer. This is a simple example that shows that
     GMO's can be beneficial to our food.

129. **Saying that chicken soup cures a cold is
     simply an old wives' tale.**
     This remedy sounds so simple, you'd think it
     can't be true. Surely medication would be better.
     But chicken soup is overloaded with amino acids
     and anti-inflammatory enzymes. Many foods are
     as well, but chicken soup is very easy to eat if you
     have a sore throat and it's easily digestible. The
     acids in chicken soup are incredibly effective
     against any respiratory infections, chest
     infections and bronchial infections.

130. **Honey is a very primitive way to cure a cough.**
     This is another old wives' tale that turns out to be
     true. Honey is more effective than
     dextromethorphan (the ingredient that's in every
     over-the-counter cold and cough medicine.)

131. **Cheese gives you nightmares.**
     It's easier to drift to sleep and you sleep more
     peacefully if you consume cheese.

132. **MSG causes headaches.**

In my first book, I mentioned that Chinese food isn't that bad for you (It is still considered by readers to be the best misconception I have ever debunked.)

MSG has no negative side effects so long as it's eaten in reasonable portions.

133. **Artificial sweeteners are a good substitute for sugar.**

Sugar has 16 calories per teaspoon.

Sweeteners have no calories.

But studies have shown that sweeteners cause people to put on weight. It is still unclear why but two separate studies validated this.

The San Antonio Heart Study observed 3,500 adults for eight years during the 1980s and noticed that the majority of their BMI's rose.

The American Cancer society did a similar test with 80,000 women over a year.

The study showed that those that had artificial sweeteners instead of sugar always tended to put on weight.

134. **You have eaten soy sauce.**

Soy sauce takes ages to make and it is too easy to make a soy substitute that lasts much longer. Most soy sauce you have eaten is a concoction of caramel coloring, salt, corn syrup (that's popular with food imitations) and hydrolyzed vegetable proteins.

135. Honey pots contain honey.

Most industries get their honey from China. A lot of Chinese honey has its pollen filtered out and replaced with corn syrup and sweeteners.

You might think, "Okay, it's diluted honey but it's still technically honey, right?"

According to the FDA, honey must contain pollen. Over 75% of the honey they tested from America didn't have a trace of pollen.

So you have probably consumed honey 25% as often as you thought you did.

The only way to guarantee you're eating pure honey is to stick your hand in a beehive. Good luck with that.

136. You have used olive oil.

Most olive oil is either heavily diluted or a complete forgery. Diluted oil is usually composed of 80% sunflower oil and 20% olive.

Fake olive oil is a vast business in the mob. It's too hard to make and too easy to fake. (I didn't mean for that to rhyme.) Fake olive farms were found in South Italy in 2008. There wasn't just one fake farm. There were ninety. Ninety farms producing fake olive oil and that's just one country in one year.

There were two Spanish people arrested for selling hundreds of thousands of liters of "olive oil" this year.

There is so much business in fake olive oil that it's impossible to tell how much real oil we are actually consuming but it is definitely a lot less than we think.

137.   You have eaten saffron spice.
Saffron is considered to be the greatest spice in the world. It is such a delicacy that people actually brag when they have consumed it.

Except they probably haven't. Nearly all saffron spice is a substitute (made of jelly) or a diluted version with only 10% saffron.

138.   Dark bread is healthier than white bread.
Most dark bread is made of the same white flour as white bread (the color comes from a molasses or caramel dye.)

If you want healthy bread, you need to buy 100% whole wheat or whole-grain wheat for extra fiber.

139.   The McDonalds' ketchup containers are too small.
A lot of consumers don't know that the ketchup containers at McDonalds can be opened so you can put at least five times more ketchup in it. If you don't eat fast food, you will find this fact trivial.

If you do eat fast food, this fact will change your life.

140.   The salmon that you buy in stores is naturally pink.
The pinkness comes from a dye. Salmons are only pink when they are in their natural environment. 95% of the salmon we eat is harvested in salmon farms so they lose their pink color and turn grey.

141. Cheddar cheese is bright orange.
Cheddar has no defining color. It can be white, yellow, brown, orange, and even green. To simplify it, they added a dye so consumers can easily identify which cheeses are cheddar.

142. Kobe beef is common.
Kobe beef is considered to be the finest beef in the world (it costs about £50 per kilo.) However, any restaurant that claims to serve Kobe beef is lying.

The FDA insisted that Kobe beef failed to fit their terms as a healthy food and so it is illegal to sell it.

The only place in the world that you can get it is Japan (and even then, it is incredibly difficult.)

143. Sausages can be naturally red.
Red sausages seem more appetizing than brown sausages but that redness comes from a dye called E128 (also known as Red 2G.)

But who cares if it's dyed? It's not like that dye gives you cancer or anything.

Oh wait. It does. Test mice have been injected with this dye and they have contracted cancer. More research is being done on this chemical but it would be best to avoid red sausages just to be safe.

Remember, the red dye doesn't affect the taste, just the color. So there is no advantage in eating these types of sausages.

144. France has the highest consumption of cheese.
Despite the fact that cheese is often associated
with France, Greece has the highest cheese
consumption.

145. Crusts don't have any nutrients.
Many parents have told their children to eat the
crust of their sandwich because "it's the best
part" when they just want them to finish their
meal. But this can't be right because the crust
comes from the same dough as the rest of the
bread, right?

But in reality, crust has far more
antioxidants than the rest of the bread. This is
because bread undergoes the Maillard reaction
when it is baked which shoves 88% of the
enzymes into the crust. What kind of enzymes?
Pronyl-lysine.

You know what that does? Beats the hell out
of cancer. Seriously. It skyrockets your body's
cancer prevention points (CPP.)

**146. Spinach doesn't have as much iron as we
thought.**
Okay, this one is a double misconception. The
idea that spinach has tons of iron has been
popularized by Popeye.

But a recent idea has been circulating the
Internet that when somebody put the iron
content on the ingredients, a decimal point was
misplaced giving the false impression that
spinach has ten times more iron than it actually
has.

This was intended as a joke by the British Medical Journal in 1981 but was taken seriously.

147. Table salt increases blood pressure.

Not having enough salt is more dangerous than having too much salt. The human body needs 1.5g of salt per day to function. It's a requirement just like protein, carbs and fats. It's true that salt will increase your blood pressure if you have over 6g per day (an average in the U.S. is 3.4g) so it's quite difficult to consume too much salt daily. But if you have less than the required 1.5g per day, it is more likely your blood pressure will increase.

148. Fish oil prevents heart disease because it is full of Omega-3.

These yellow pellets have become very popular with nutritionists recently. This idea comes from the "Eskimo diet" from the Inuit tribes who eat mostly fish and rarely succumb to heart disease. But the reason why Inuits don't die from heart disease is because they usually die from the cold. Outside of badly researched Eskimo diets, there's little evidence to support this theory. Fish oil isn't bad for you, but it's not going to have an effect on your heart, for better or for worse.

<u>HARRY POTTER</u>

149.   Harry Potter's parents were in their thirties when they died.

> In the book, James and Lily Potter were only twenty-one when they perished. This is confirmed in the Deathly Hallows when Harry visits their grave.

150.   In Harry Potter, the Ravenclaw symbol is a raven.

> According to Pottermore, the bird is an eagle.

151.   In Harry Potter, Snape is a vampire.

> This sounds like a silly fan theory (and that is exactly what it is) but it became so popular, that Harry Potter's author, JK Rowling, had to disprove it herself.

152.   In the Harry Potter books, Death Eaters and Aurors can fly.

> In the books, only Snape and Voldermort can fly. The number one reason movies change things from the books they are based on is because "it looks cool."

153.   In the first book, the snake that Harry Potter releases from the zoo becomes Voldermort's pet, Nagini.

> The zoo snake is described as a constrictor (which is not venomous.) Nagini, on the other hand, is extremely venomous.

154. In Harry Potter and the Goblet of Fire, Durmstrang is an all boys school and Beauxbatons is an all girls school.

It seems that way in the film to simplify the plot, but it is not the case in the book.

155. Children are accepted into Hogwarts when they turn eleven.

Fans believe this because Harry opens his acceptance letter on his eleventh birthday. But fans forget that this is simply the first letter he sees. His evil uncle destroyed the other letters.

156. There are seven horcruxes containing seven pieces of Voldermort's soul.

There are eight.
i)   Professor Quirrel
ii)   Tom Riddle's diary
iii) Marvolo's Gaunt ring
iv)   Salazar Slytherin's locket
v)   Helga Hufflepuff's cup
vi)   Rowena Ravenclaw's diadem
vii) Nagini the snake
viii) Some guy called Harry Potter

157. JK Rowling told Alan Rickman everything about his character, Severus Snape, when he started filming the first movie.

Alan Rickman knew there was more to Snape than meets the eye but he had no idea of his character's true role in the story until years later.

158. **JK Rowling told a girl that she would have a part in the Harry Potter films if she beat her anorexia.**

That's not how casting decisions work. Also, JK Rowling isn't the casting director.

A young anorexic girl called Evanna Lynch wrote to JK Rowling about her passion for Harry Potter and discussed her illness but there was never a mention in the letters about her being cast in the movie.

Three years later, Evanna beat her illness and got cast in Harry Potter as Luna Lovegood, unbeknownst to Rowling.

<u>HISTORY</u>

159.   Ancient Egyptians were obsessed with death.
Ancient Egyptians seemed to be obsessed with death because WE are obsessed with how they perceived death. They would probably think our culture is obsessed with funny cat videos. A lot of Ancient Egyptian culture revolved around farming, hunting and fishing but nobody cares about that. They didn't think and talk about death 24/7. Death is a big part of every culture. Their concept of it seems so fascinating because it is so different from ours.

160.   In Ancient Egypt, slaves were buried with the Pharaohs.
Of the three hundred Pharaohs known, only two Pharaohs buried their slaves with them.

161.   Hieroglyphs were used for spells and curses.
The Mummy movies have popularized this but it's untrue.

162.   We have uncovered all of Egypt's ancient relics.
Archeologists are still finding artifacts from Ancient Egypt. Everybody knows about pyramids and mummies and tombs. But did you know that a solar boat was found in the Great Pyramid recently? It was designed to allow deceased Pharaohs to help the sun god, Ra fight demons.

163. Ancient Egyptians invented hieroglyphics.
It is unknown which country invented hieroglyphics but they made their way to Egypt from West Asia.

164. All the Egyptian pyramids are covered in hieroglyphics.
Almost every single room within the pyramids is utterly undecorated.

165. Ancient Egypt enslaved millions of Israelites.
Outside the Bible, there has never been a single document to suggest that Ancient Egypt enslaved the Jewish populace.

166. Ancient Egyptians were dark-skinned.
When Ridley Scott released his film, Exodus: Gods and Kings, many people criticized how white actors were playing Ancient Egyptians.

The problem with this argument is that nobody knows what Ancient Egyptians looked like. Artistic depictions of Egyptians use color to signify status rather than literal skin color – men were brown, women were white, some were painted red or black depending on which god they worshipped, etc.

Pieces of information conflicts with each other. Forensic artist, Frank Domingo confirmed that the Sphinx is based on a black woman.

However, DNA tests have validated that the Pharaoh, Ramses II, was redheaded. These two facts would suggest a mixed culture but the truth is we just don't know for sure.

167. All Ancient Egyptians shaved their entire bodies.

Only the nobles shaved themselves.

168. There are more people alive today than ever before in history.

Calculations show that there have been approximately 106 billion people since 50,000 BC. There are slightly over 7 billion people alive today.

169. Life expectancy used to be very low until the last century.

It is true that we are living longer than ever before but society has an idea that elderly people in the past were exceptionally rare.

This misconception is because infant mortality rates were way higher up until a century ago. So if one person died at the age of one and another person died at the age of eighty, the average age of death for these two people is forty. Since the infant mortality rate is way lower nowadays, it appears that life expectancy has drastically increased.

The mortality rate in medieval times wasn't great but it was nowhere near as bad as often depicted in films. 50% of people lived to twenty-one. But once a person got over the age of thirty, about 70% of them lived to their seventies.

Living to eighty or ninety hasn't been that uncommon for millennia. The Ancient Greek philosopher, Plato, playwright, Sophocles, and Pharaoh, Ramses, all died at eighty.

170. All gladiators were men.
Female gladiators (called gladiatrixes) fought in the Coliseum.

171. In medieval times, people used to bang goblets of wine together before they drank them just in case they were poisoned.
Let's create a scenario – I'm drinking from a goblet of wine with a friend (typical Friday night) and he poisons my wine. If we bang our goblets together, droplets of wine would pour into both goblets meaning that the poison will be in both drinks. If you trusted the person you were having a drink with, you would clink your drinks together because you knew the other person would never poison you.

This is a fantastic idea but the truth is sadly, far less interesting. The clinking of glasses is meant to symbolize the "unity of senses."

We have five official senses – sight, taste, smell, touch, and hearing.

Smelling the wine is using one sense. Tasting it is using another sense. Looking at your friend whom you are having the drink with is using your sight. And the clinking of the glasses is using the sense of touch and hearing.

But if anyone asks me where clinking comes from, I just tell them the goblet story. It's more interesting.

172. The Queen of England says, "Arise sir_____."
No queen of England has been known to do this.

173. A cow caused the Great Chicago Fire.
After the fire in 1871, the Chicago tribune publicized the "fact" that the fire was caused by a cow that knocked a lit lantern while it was being milked. Michael Ahern admitted decades later that he fabricated the story.

174. The Spanish Inquisition caused millions of deaths.
It is assumed that The Inquisition killed everyone who was accused of heresy.

However, most people who were accused were acquitted or had their sentences suspended.

According to historian Thomas Madden, "the Inquisition was widely hailed as the best-run, most humane court in Europe." Some prisoners would intentionally blaspheme to get out of the state prisons and be put into the Inquisition prisons.

Over time, English Protestants heavily exaggerated the brutality of the Inquisition. The Inquisition led to approximately 1,250 deaths in total. That is still horrific but a thousand times less than historians originally believed.

175. Only white people had black slaves.
Throughout history, white people are always seen as the oppressors of the enslaved black community. But between the 16th-18th century, Africans enslaved 1.5 million white Europeans in the Barbary slave trade. In fact, white people were the first to stop slavery in modern times. Slavery still continues in Africa to this day.

176. The Emancipation Proclamation freed the slaves.

> The Proclamation was only for the states that were rebelling against the Union. It didn't affect the States that were loyal to President Lincoln.

177. Stonehenge is the oldest human construction.

> Gobekli Tepe in Turkey is 6,000 years older than Stonehenge. It dates back to 9,000 BC and is thought to be the oldest human construction. It was formed during the Stone Age and predates agriculture.

178. Iron maidens were a torture device that looked like a coffin and the closing lid had spikes on the inside to impale whoever was in it.

> This was first seen in a painting. You would probably recognize it from the beginning of Batman Returns. It never existed.

179. The "rule of thumb" meant that in medieval times, you could legally beat your wife with a stick if it had less girth than your thumb.

> There's no evidence from any historical law or legal research to support this claim.

180. Our ancestors only ate meat.

> Our ancestors diet was known as the Paleo Diet. The Paleo Diet was thought to consist only of meat. However, our ancestors ate bread, seeds, nuts, berries, roots, and grass 30,000 years ago.

181. Women used to protest by burning bras.

I'm sure a group of women did here and there but there was no defined location or group or year.

182. The Mona Lisa background was brown.

The background has gone brown from old age. When it was originally painted, the background behind the Mona Lisa was a very bright blue.

183. The Scottish hero, William Wallace was known as Braveheart.

The name "Braveheart" was given to the king, Robert the Bruce. You know. The guy who betrayed William Wallace, which led to his horrific death. And they named the film after that villain.

Also, Scots didn't wear kilts back then.
Did that movie do anything right?

184. The Hindenburg was filled with helium.

Many believe that the Hindenburg exploded because a spark combusted the helium within the Hindenburg. And that was exactly what happened... apart from one difference.

It was hydrogen, not helium.

185. No one survived the Hindenburg crash.

Ninety-seven passengers were on the Hindenburg blimp when it exploded. Only thirty-five of them were killed in the crash (and one more died when the Hindenburg fell on him.)

186. Samurais have defended their country to the death for centuries.

Samurais were known for following "the way of the warrior." This code of the samurai was known as "Bushido."

Samurais were considered the greatest soldiers of Japan and were so proud of their nation that they would commit hari-kiri (slice their own belly) if they ever faced defeat. They would die by their own hands rather than bring shame to their Emperor.

But samurais were not uncompromiseable warriors that would die for their country. They were just people. They killed for money. They killed their employers if they didn't get paid enough. They would betray their Emperor and switch sides if it worked to their advantage. Samurais were portrayed as noble warriors as a marketing campaign to make Japan look awesome.

And it worked.

187. In medieval times, civilians would say, "Bless you" when a person sneezed because they thought it was the soul attempting to escape the body.

When the Black Death was killing millions of Europeans, people noticed that the first symptom was sneezing.

Crying out, "Bless you" was a desperate plea to let God spare a life.

188. **Vikings placed their dead on rafts and burned them at sea.**

Despite what the movie, Thor: The Dark World depicted, Vikings buried their dead normally. Who would have ever thought that a Thor movie would be inaccurate?

189. **Hitler rose to power by brainwashing all of Germany.**

Hitler only received 30% of the vote when he ran for office. In the runoff, he got 37%. His opponent was Paul von Hindenburg. He received 53% of the vote even though he was not interested in a second term. He only ran in the first place because he really didn't want Hitler in office.

190. **Women weren't able to vote until the 1920s.**

Lily Maxwell was the first woman to vote back in 1867. When she voted, it wasn't illegal for women to do so. It would be like if a cat was elected to be mayor. There is no law against it. (That's not a stupid example. There is a cat Mayor called Stubbs in Alaska. Please research it to prove I'm not making that up.)

Now where was I?

Oh yeah. Women voting.

You may wonder why women didn't vote if it wasn't illegal? Back then, women weren't expected to have experience in diplomacy, construction, military, shipping, banking, etc. However, Maxwell was a shop owner with her own property and she had an excellent understanding of business. This got the attention of other businesswomen who also voted. When this got the attention of men in power, only then did they make it illegal for women to vote. It was this incident that kickstarted the Suffragettes movement which had to fight for decades to get back their right to vote. Oh men! Why did they stop women from voting? Hold on...

191. Men were against women voting.

History books have simplified the Suffragettes story so it sounds like Women Vs Men. No legal or political debate is ever that black and white.

Many men supported the Suffragettes and many women were against them. Women believed that the Suffragettes might tarnish how society viewed their gender and that they should "know their place."

20,000 men were involved in the National Men's League in 1912 which heavily supported the Suffragettes. Even former slave turned politician, Frederick Douglas (who had been persecuted for his skin color) fought for women to be given the same rights he was often denied.

192. The Olympic torch relay has been around since the beginning of the Olympics.

In Ancient Greece, the torch would burn during the Olympic Games.

But the torch relay where representatives carry the torch from Greece to the Olympic Games has only existed since 1936.

193.   Napoleon had his men shoot the noses off the Sphinx of Egypt.

Napoleon didn't invade Egypt until 1798. We have known the Sphinx's nose has been missing since at least 1738 when a Danish explorer named Frederic Louis Norden drew the noseless Sphinx when he passed by it. The missing nose was caused by weather erosion.

194.   Pythagoras came up with Pythagoras' theorem.

If your mathematic knowledge is a bit rusty, Pythagoras theorem was an equation to figure out the angle of a triangle. However, the Babylonians were the first to use this theorem a millennium before Pythagoras was born. The Egyptians, Chinese and Indians used it long before Pythagoras did.

195.   Mussolini made the trains run on time.

The trains ran more efficiently before and after his intervention. HIS train was the only train that ran on time. This inaccurate idea became popular because Mussolini prided himself on how punctual his (and only his) train were.

196.   Michelangelo was the most famous painter of his time.

Despite the fact that he painted the Sistine Chapel, Michelangelo's legacy was in being a sculptor. Speaking of the Sistine Chapel...

197. The Sistine Chapel is huge.

Before I was thrown out of the Sistine Chapel (don't ask why,) I was astonished by how small the building was. It's far smaller than a church. Its dimensions are 40 x 13 x 21 meters. (I measured it. I had a lot of free time after I got thrown out.) You can see the entire interior without walking around. The chapel itself looks surprisingly dull. From the outside, it looks like a boring, brown building. Based on its outward appearance, you would never assume it houses one of the world's most famous paintings.

198. The United Kingdom has only recently become a multicultural society.

Britain has had black citizens for over 1,800 years. I don't mean slaves. Tombs of wealthy Africans have been uncovered in the UK recently that are over a millennium old.

In 1501, Catherine of Aragon brought over Muslims, Jews and Africans. Although Britain is more multicultural than ever, all ethnicities have lived freely in the UK for centuries.

199. Pirates stole gold.

Pirates stole soap, candles, household supplies, sewing tools, food, salted fish, navigational tools, gunpowder, and medical supplies a lot more than gold.

200. Anne Boleyn had eleven fingers.

Some reports say she had eleven toes but both statements aren't true.

201. Judo has existed for thousands of years.
Kano Jigoro created Judo in the 1880s.

202. Black belts have existed for thousands of years.
That was Kano too. Before black belts, martial artists were rewarded with scrolls for their hard work. Kano's belt concept became popular because it showed the rank of each fighter as they fought.

203. Black belt fighters are martial art experts.
If you obtain a black belt, that means you have completed the first step of your training. This rank is known as Shodan. This takes an average of 4.5 years to obtain.

But that's the first level. There are ten levels! It would take literally a lifetime to reach level ten for you to be considered an "expert." But by then, you'll be about seventy so who's going to fight you?

204. Financial bank collapses have only happened in the past century.
We have suffered many bank crashes in the last hundred years - The Great Depression of the beginning of the 20th century, The Wall Street crash in the 1980s and The Financial Crisis of 2008.

Throughout history, there have obviously been many financial crises caused by war and natural disasters but never by banks.

Oh wait. There has been.

The Florentine banking collapse of 1345 was the earliest mass financial crisis on record. And it was catalyzed not by war or flooding but from something as mundane as bad loans and under-regulation (just like the modern financial crises.) This bankrupted most farmers in Europe leading to a continental famine killing millions.

So if you lost your job during the 2008 crisis, it could've been worse.

205. If JFK wasn't assassinated, America never would've invaded Vietnam.

If JFK wasn't murdered, he would have been dead within a year or at the very least, had to step down from the Presidency.

JFK is often known as the most handsome US President. Many people describe him the same way – he had a natural glow about him. It was true that JFK had a distinctive color. It is one of the side effects of Addison's disease, which Kennedy suffered from. Addison's disease causes damage to the adrenal glands discoloring the skin to a bronze color. This is why Kennedy always looked bronze. It wasn't because he was healthy. He was dying. He had to be rushed to the hospital nine times between 1955 and 1957.

This was a well-known fact in the Presidential circle which dilutes the conspiracy theory that the American government killed JFK. Why would they assassinate him if they knew he was at death's door?

206. JFK was against the invasion of Vietnam.
The conspiracy theory revolving around JFK is
simple – the government assassinated Kennedy
because they wanted to go to Vietnam but JFK
was against it. The government supposedly killed
him so they could declare war on Vietnam.
But JFK had already begun sending advisers and
Special Forces to Vietnam before his death. It
wasn't a full-scale war but he directly began
military activity in South Vietnam. He didn't want
a war but he knew it was unavoidable.

**207. The Founding Fathers of America were
fundamentally Christian.**
America seems a lot more cosmopolitan
nowadays, not just with ethnicities but with
religions. The U.S. now has a mix of Christians,
Muslims, and Hindus. You would imagine things
were different back in George Washington's time
when everybody was Christian.

Not so. The Founding Fathers greatly
admired the Muslim faith. John Adams and
Benjamin Rush regularly hailed the Islamic
prophet, Muhammad. Thomas Jefferson taught
himself Arabic with his own Quran. Benjamin
Franklin wanted every child to know the
teachings of Confucius and Muhammad. And
some guy called George Washington had Muslims
work for him because he found them friendly,
intelligent and passionate.

208. **Ancient Rome had epic parties and banquets.**
Some history books say that Romans regularly ate until they vomited. They supposedly had vomiting rooms at their banquets. Many depictions of Roman banquets on television will show a room filled with an immeasurable amount of food and wine. However, Roman laws were tight about banquet budgets. If there was too much food, it was likely some of it would rot. The empire couldn't risk their soldiers suffering from food poisoning and would never waste a large amount of food. Julius Caesar was the strictest regulator of these laws and would often stop banquets that he believed were overindulgent.

HUMAN BODY

209. A human baby is weak.
Considering how small a newborn baby is, it can find its way to its mother by crawling with one hand. You do realize that when your newborn baby does this, it's basically moving its body while doing one-armed push-ups simultaneously?!

If a baby grabbed onto a horizontal pole one-handed, it would be able to keep up its entire body weight. Most adults can't do this. Pound for pound, a baby is stronger than a fully-grown ox.

210. You should wash your face with soap to prevent acne.
Washing your face with soap can remove protective oils on your skin, which can increase acne.

211. Your blood is blue. It becomes red when it is exposed to oxygen. That's why your veins look blue.
This bizarre misconception has become popular recently. I've never heard of this idea until two years ago and now I hear of it every few weeks even though it's utter nonsense.

212. If you don't wash your hair, you will get lice.
Washing your hair will not stop lice from taking up residence in your head. All you need to do to catch lice is be near someone else with lice.

213. If you can't sleep, just sit in bed and eventually you will fall asleep.

As soon as you feel like you can't sleep, get out of bed and go to a different room and do a simple activity like read a book. Make sure the light in this room is not too dark or too bright. Once you start to feel tired again (in about twenty minutes) return to bed and you should fall asleep with ease.

214. Your brain isn't as active when you are asleep.

According Medicine at Harvard Medical School, "During some stages of sleep, the brain is just as active as when we are fully awake." Your brain never has a rest. Only your body does.

215. Dreaming happens when you are in REM (rapid-eye moving) sleep.

REM is when your dreams seem the most vivid and these are the dreams you are most likely to remember but you can dream during any stage of sleep.

216. If you die in a dream, you die in real life.

Okay, we are not in The Matrix (probably) so this is a ludicrous claim. Even if this was true, how could anyone know this? How could any researcher know what a person was dreaming if they died before they had a chance to tell anybody?

Also, people do have dreams where they die. It's not that uncommon.

217. **If you train yourself to sleep less, you will get used to it.**
I'm certain every parent on Earth will disagree with this when they have a newborn baby. Your body has only a handful of basic needs but sleep is one of them. If you deprive yourself of sleep, you will not be able to function. If you slept every day for five hours, you would never get used to it no matter how much time went by.

218. **Counting sheep helps you sleep (and rhymes.)**
This doesn't work because you need to concentrate in order to count. Going to sleep only happens when you allow yourself to relax. If you are concentrating on something, even on a task as silly as counting sheep, it's not going to help.

219. **You can tell if someone is dead by feeling his or her pulse.**
Doctors don't do this at a hospital to check if someone has died (in spite of what movies show you.)
Using a stethoscope to verify a heartbeat is the most sensible technique.

220. **Viruses stay alive on hard surfaces for ages.**
There's a misconception that viruses can survive for days on a hard surface but it's inaccurate.
Most viruses die with 2-8 hours.
A cold is the only common virus that lives for 24 hours.

221. You should survive if your hand was cut off.
Characters on television and in movies often survive after having a limb cut off (especially in Game of Thrones.)

In reality, it's rare to survive losing a limb. You would only survive if you immediately applied pressure to the wound and not move at all (which is really hard when you're in agony and your body is going into shock.) You have sixty seconds at most to seal the wound before your body loses consciousness. If you do all of this perfectly, your odds of survival are still not great.

222. If you get knocked out, you'll wake up a few hours later with a headache.
If you are knocked out for longer than five minutes, it's likely you will have a concussion and you need to see a doctor urgently or you may suffer a life-threatening brain injury.

223. You should brush your teeth immediately after you eat.
Brushing straight after food can cause extreme damage to tooth enamel. Acidity in foods cause enamel to soften so you shouldn't expose your teeth to it.

You should actually brush BEFORE you eat and focus on the gums rather than the teeth.

224. Pregnancy lasts nine months.
9 months is 36 weeks. Pregnancy normally lasts slightly over 38 weeks.

225. A pregnant woman is eating for two.
This sounds like a pregnant woman should double her portions. Doctors advise pregnant women to eat an extra 340 calories during their second trimester and an extra 452 calories during her third trimester.

226. Pregnant women can't fly during their final trimester.
This misconception has become popularized by the television show, Friends when Phoebe couldn't fly when she was carrying triplets.

Protocols vary from airline to airline but the reason heavily pregnant women are advised not to fly has nothing to do with the plane being bad for the baby. It is simply because air attendants don't want to risk the possibility of a woman going into early labor on a plane.

227. Spicy food triggers labor.
This is another misconception popularized by Friends. In the show, Rachel is encouraged to eat spicy food to accelerate her pregnancy. An expert called Jonathan Shafford concluded that women have little or no control over their pregnancy.

228. Pregnant women shouldn't be near a cat.
It's totally fine for a pregnant woman to stroke a cat. But it is heavily advised for pregnant women not to go near their litter box as it could have parasites in its droppings that could be harmful to the unborn child.

229. Pregnant women shouldn't eat sushi.
Sushi is fine if you are pregnant. The reason
doctors advise you not to eat it is to avoid the risk
of food poisoning since certain bacteria can be
found in uncooked meats.

230. Pregnant women shouldn't eat fish.
Fish are very nutritious for a pregnant woman
and consuming them should be encouraged.
Some fish have too much mercury, which can be
dangerous for you if you are pregnant. However,
these are more obscure fish like swordfish,
marlin or shark. Are you going to eat shark
anytime soon? No? Then you're fine. The only
common fish you should avoid is tuna.

231. Pregnant women shouldn't drink coffee.
Obviously a pregnant woman shouldn't drink
tons of coffee but a mild amount every now and
again is completely harmless.

232. Men think of sex every seven seconds.
How would men drive? Or eat? Or do anything?
Experts estimate that 30% of men don't think
about sex during the day at all.

**233. Your heart will stop pumping once it is
disconnected to your body.**
Although your heart is extremely important, its
purpose and design is pretty simple. It pumps
blood. That's it. The heart has its own electrical
impulse so it can keep pumping so long as it's
receiving oxygen.

234. Acupuncture is a pseudoscience.
Although the idea that acupuncture helps your life energy (chi) is considered an old-fashioned idea, acupuncture is still effective. When the needles are inserted into your skin, your body naturally activates a chemical called adenosine which is similar to an anesthetic. Acupuncture is especially effective with migraines.

235. The bigger your brain, the smarter you are.
Your brain size doesn't determine your overall intelligence. Oliver Cromwell had the largest brain on record and that guy was kind of a jerk.

It's hard to define what "smart" is as everyone is good at certain things and bad at others.

<u>INVENTIONS</u>

236. Apple invented the tablet.
The first tablet was the Gridpad. Grid systems invented it in 1989. It didn't sell well because it cost $3,000. (I say that as if tablets aren't overpriced now.)

237. Rockets were invented in the last century.
The Chinese Navy used multi-stage rockets in the 14th century. And when I say "rocket," I don't mean a firecracker. It had booster rockets that would propel it into the air. It was very basic and could fly less than 200m in the air but it's pretty impressive since this was a century before Columbus came to America.

238. Arrest warrants are a recent concept.
The Vikings used arrest warrants over a thousand years ago and it was a surprisingly complex legal system. They had regular public law gatherings to catalogue the crimes committed and to have them rectified with fines or settlements.

239. Child support is a recent concept.
The Vikings created this as well. A 12th century Icelandic legal code called the Gragas stipulated a system to support a child after divorce. The system was surprisingly thorough for its time and both spouses were expected to contribute to the child (or children's) upbringing according to their wealth and/or ability to work.

240. Welfare has existed for hundreds of years.
The Vikings invented this too. The Gragas outlined a tax system guaranteeing care of the poor if their families couldn't provide for them (if the recipient didn't live in Iceland.)

241. Air conditioning is a recent invention.
2,500 years ago, Persians built complex irrigation systems called qanats that transported water underground. 1,000 years ago, Persians started to build wind towers over their buildings. The wind would flow into the qanats, which would circle the cool air back.

242. Post offices are a recent invention.
The Persians invented postal offices in 500 BC.

243. Chewing gum is a recent invention.
Chewing gum has existed for 5,000 years, all the way back in the Neolithic age. The oldest gum ever found was found in Finland and was made out of birch bark tar. This gum was antiseptic so it was probably used to eradicate gum infections.

244. Crosswords have existed for centuries.
Crosswords are such simple puzzles, you would imagine someone invented them hundreds, perhaps even thousands of years ago.

But no. Arthur Wynne invented the crossword in 1913.

245. CPR has been used to revive people for centuries.

CPR was invented in 1960 by Dr. James Elam and Peter Safar.

246. Fast food is a recent invention.

Fast food began in Ancient Rome. Romans weren't able to afford decent cooking equipment so they would often rely on quick, cheap meals. Fast-food shops existed in Rome in 113 AD.

247. Dentistry has existed for centuries.

More like millennia. Dentistry has been practiced for over 9,000 years in Pakistan.

Sadly, this was before anesthetics. The best painkiller they had on offer at the time was good old-fashioned alcohol. And speaking of teeth...

248. Dentures have existed for centuries.

Like dentistry, dentures have existed for millennia (approximately 700 BC) in Etruria (ancient Italy.)

249. Toothbrushes have existed for centuries.

The Chinese invented toothbrushes in 3,000 BC.

250. "Twerking" was invented recently.

Miley Cyrus did not invent this ridiculous dance. "Twerk" can be found in the Oxford English Dictionary since 1820.

251. Roller skates were invented in the 1960s.

A Belgian inventor called John Joseph Merlin invented skates in the 1760s.

252. Self-driving cars are a recent invention.
S. Tsugawa invented the VaMoRs self-driving car in 1987. It could drive at 55mph for 12 miles. That doesn't sound impressive but Tsugawa just wanted to see if it could work conceptually before drastically boosting its abilities.

In 1994, his new VaMP could detect other vehicles, know what lane it was in, recognize road signs and change lanes accordingly.

Unfortunately, Tsugawa didn't have 82 bajillion dollars so the self-driving car wasn't mass-produced until recently by Google.

253. Newspapers didn't exist until 1440.
Okay, if you know your history, it seems impossible for newspapers to exist before 1440 because that was the year Johannes Gutenberg invented the printing press. So how could newspapers be printed any earlier?

Because the Chinese created their newspapers on sheets (called tipao,) and copied them by hand enough times so there was one for each imperial officer. Citizens would flock to these officers to see the latest news. There obviously couldn't be enough so most people had to share the newspapers or learn from word-of-mouth.

254. The seismograph (earthquake measurer) has only existed for a century.
The first seismograph dates back to 132 AD in China. It was a large bronze cauldron with eight dragonheads with balls in their mouths on its

exterior (seriously, I'm not making that up.) The dragonheads were attached to a column within. A tremor would cause the column to wobble.

Depending on where the tremor was coming from, one of the dragonheads would drop its ball, which would tell seismographers which direction the earthquake was coming from.

255. Selfie sticks are a recent invention.
Hiroshi Ueda invented the selfie stick in 1983. It didn't sell well and has only become popular recently (even though it looks ridiculous.)

256. The first invention to break the sound barrier was the fighter jet.
If you're clever, you may think the answer is the whip.

But that's wrong too. The answer is... crunchy food.

The snap you hear from biting into a carrot, a crunchy bar or a peanut is actually a sonic boom. That sound is moving at 300 meters per second so it breaks the sound barrier.

257. James Dyson invented bladeless fans in 2009.
Tokyo Shiba's Electric company invented this fan in 1981 but it couldn't get the funding to mass produce it.

258. E-cigarettes are a recent invention.
Herbert Gilbert invented the e-cigarette in 1963. It was considered healthier than the e-cigarettes of today because it used a battery to generate heat

rather than a chemical. Sadly, all chemical, tobacco and pharmaceutical companies turned him down for the same reason – money. These companies were already making billions and didn't need to change it up or risk turning Gilbert into a competitor, taking away their business.

259. High heels are a recent trend.

Persians invented high heels a thousand years ago... for men. Horseback archers would wear them to help them secure themselves in stirrups while firing their weapon. As high-heeled archers became feared, Persian men would wear them to show off authority. For this reason, they stopped being used to gain the advantage in battle but instead became a social requirement to demand respect. The taller the heels, the more authority the wearer would have. But the heels became so tall that wears would walk effeminately, which turned high heels into a female trend.

260. Drones are a recent invention.

Archibald Low invented the first drone in 1916 to help in World War I. It was mostly made out of wood and tin and could be controlled by a radio. It wasn't successful as its own engine interfered with its radio.

261. Head-mounted computer displays like Google Glass are a recent invention.

The first computer glasses were invented in 1961. They were very basic and they gradually became more advanced over the decades. By 1980, Steve

Mann created computer glasses called the WearComp that could wirelessly communicate with other computers and were even able to share videos.

262. **The odometer was invented at the same time as the car.**

The odometer measures how much your car has travelled. Although the car is a recent invention, Vitruvius invented the odometer in approximately 25 BC. Some historians debate that Archimedes invented it even earlier than that but the point is that invention was millennia ago, not centuries.

So how did Vitruvius invent the odometer thousands of years before the car? He worked out that a chariot wheel would turn 400 times every time the chariot would travel a mile. He built an axle within the chariot that would drop a stone into a box every time the wheel turned 400 times. So after a long journey, if Vitruvius counted ten stones in the box, he would know he had travelled ten miles.

263. **Spray tan has existed for about twenty years.**
Fake tan the way we know it today, has existed since the 1960s. It was available at gas stations where customers would spray themselves with a tanning hose.

<u>LAW</u>

264. Medicinal marijuana has only been legal recently.

Marijuana has been used for medicinal purposes in China since 4,000 BC. It was legal throughout most of the world until 1937 until media publisher, William Randolph Hearst condemned it in his newspapers, which inevitably led to its criminalization. If you recognize his name, it's because he inspired the main character in the film, Citizen Kane. He controlled the media so he destroyed that movie, forcing it to lose millions.

That's right. Hearst ruined what is considered to be the greatest film ever made and criminalized marijuana. He was clearly a supervillain.

265. Smoking bans are a recent law.

The European Catholic Church created smoking bans in the 1600s. If you were caught smoking near a church during this time, you would be barred from going to Heaven. Depending on your beliefs, this punishment was either too extreme or non-existent.

The ban was a tad more severe in China. In 1639, Emperor Chongzhen sentenced any smoker to death. And if you think that's extreme, the following emperor changed the law so that anyone possessing tobacco was to be killed. And people complain that smoking bans are too strict nowadays.

266.   Drawing on a dollar bill is against the law.
You can't cut or burn dollar bills but you can draw little doodles on them.

267.   There is one person headlining every crime inspection.
In every detective show, from CSI to True Detective, it always seems like there are one or two people in charge of nearly everything.

In the show, Dexter, the main character collects DNA for the Miami police force and analyses it. In reality, two different people would carry out these two duties. Crime scenes are extremely complex and would require as many people working on them as possible rather than shoving most of the information onto one person.

268.   You can't get convicted twice for the same crime.
This idea became famous from the movie, Double Jeopardy. In the film, a man fakes his murder and frames his wife. She goes to jail and gets out a few years later. She tracks down her husband, intending to kill him, knowing that she can't be convicted since she already completed her sentence in prison.

However, the Supreme Court of the United States has said that the person would still go to jail since criminal would be blatantly taking advantage of a loophole in the system.

269.   Driving barefoot is illegal.
It's not. It's stupid but it's not illegal.

270. **If you were sentenced to death and you managed to survive, you would be set free.**

There is this Internet rumor suggesting that if you survived the electric chair, being hung or being shot at by a firing squad, you would be set free. How would this work? If you killed someone, and you were hanged and you managed to survive, the person you killed is still dead. This idea is utter nonsense.

271. **Undercover police officers must identify themselves if they are asked if they are cops or they would be help accountable for entrapment.**

Entrapment is when a police officer encourages or forces someone to break the law.

It is not entrapment if the cop is dealing with a person who has been identified as carrying out criminal activities. An undercover cop must keep his identity secret to carry out his job.

272. **Police interrogations are reliable at making criminals confess to crimes.**

According to studies carried out by Kassin and Kiechel Williams, innocent people will confess to a crime they didn't commit 43% of the time if they are antagonized enough.

One of the most famous examples of this is Gerry Conlon in the Guildford Four Bombings. Even though Conlon was innocent, he and his friends confessed to killing five people with a bomb after being tortured by the police. This has been famously depicted in the film, In the Name of the Father.

273. **You need someone's permission to legally film him or her in public.**

In documentaries, you will see some people have their faces blurred out. This is because they have asked to remain anonymous. If they don't ask, then they can be filmed if they are in public surroundings.

274. **Freedom of speech exempts you from the law.**

People can say offensive things that are slanderous, homophobic, sexist, or racist but cannot be held accountable for these comments, no matter how offensive they are because of free speech.

However, there are some obvious exceptions to this. You can't yell things like "Fire" or "Bomb" in public as it would produce mass panic. If you do so, you will be held accountable to the highest degree of the law and the "free speech" argument will not be able to help you. Unsurprisingly, schools and corporations have their own rules about what can and cannot be discussed for ethical reasons or to protect the establishment.

275. **Jurors are well prepared before a trial.**

Studies have been done on jurors to see if they understood what they needed to look out for in the trial. 40% understood. Only 50% of jurors understood that the defendant doesn't need to prove himself or herself guilty and 86% of them didn't know what constitutes proof of guilt.

276. Police interrogations are depicted accurately in films and television.

I can't think of a single accurate depiction of a police interrogation. Even excellent shows like Breaking Bad and Better Call Saul's police interrogation scenes use the clichéd techniques of intimidation, manipulation, physical threats, good cop/bad cop, reverse psychology, etc.

In reality, it's very simple. If a suspect demands to have an attorney present, the interrogation must stop. If a suspect invokes his or her right to be silent, the police can't coax the suspect to speak. If a suspect doesn't know his or her rights, the police will do everything in their power to help you understand them.

It wouldn't make for a very interesting scene in a movie, but it would be portrayed accurately.

277. Doctors can't breach doctor-patient confidentiality.

You've seen this a million times on television. A police officer is looking for a patient in a hospital who happens to be a suspect in a crime. They ask doctors if they have seen the suspect. The doctor tells the officer that they are not at liberty to say because of doctor-patient confidentiality.

This is a simple tool in T.V. to add tension. But it's not true. If someone's life is in danger or a criminal activity is suspected, a doctor will give as much information as possible to help the police or it would be considered an obstruction of justice. This applies to counsellor/client confidentiality as well.

MENTAL HEALTH

278. Mental illnesses have only been treated in the past century.

The first recording of treating mental illness dates back to 1,300 BC in Mesopotamia (now known as Iraq.) Medical documents from this time detail how soldiers would experience depression and flashbacks soon after they were in engaged in battle. This is the first historical reference to PTSD (Post-traumatic stress syndrome.) Doctors would advise medication, prayer or religious offerings to find peace.

279. Autism is a genetic disorder.

Autism is a bio-neurological developmental disability. This means that autism is caused by problems in the brain's neurons, not the person's D.N.A. This is significant because it means that autism is not hereditary and cannot be passed on.

280. Autistic people are unemotional.

Autistic suffers often seem like they are disinterested in their surroundings. In reality, it is the opposite. Autistics feel more emotion than a person without autism. It's like when you are so angry or scared, that you go into a state of shock and you don't seem to react emotionally. Author and occupational therapist, Lindsey Biel helps many autistic people and she says in her research that autistics are extremely expressive with their emotions when they write them down.

281. Amnesia is accurately portrayed in movies.
Nearly everything you know about amnesia is a lie thanks to movies like the Bourne trilogy.

Almost every amnesiac character in films suffers from retrograde amnesia, which causes them to forget specific events. In reality, this sort of amnesia would have great difficulty creating new memories (like in the movie, Memento and yes, that is a real disorder called anterograde amnesia.) You can have one type or the other or both.

Amnesia in movies seems to always involve forgetting events. But amnesia can involve forgetting many things.

You could look at a banana and know how to peel it and eat it but you may not remember what it is called. Or you may remember its name but not know that you are suppose to peel it or that it is even food.

You might forget names, days of the week, how to tell a story, etc. A friend of mine suffers a type of amnesia where his brain can't remember how to perceive time. If he saw me today, he can't remember if he saw me last week or last year.

In movies, amnesia can occur with a bump on the head and their memories can be returned with another bump on the head. This doesn't work. The memories may never return and if they do, it can take years. So please don't go around and hit people suffering from brain disorders on the head.

Please don't do that.

282. Eating disorders are a female problem.
25% of anorexics and bulimics are men and 40% of binge eaters are men.

283. Only skinny people suffer from bulimia.
Underweight people are actually in the minority among bulimics.

  According to the EDF study, bulimics are usually average or above-average weight.

284. Mentally ill people know what mental illness they have.
In movies, there is a moment where a character has an epiphany and this character learns the truth – they have bipolar. Or depression. Or a split-personality. Or schizophrenia.

  But it's not that simple. Bipolar can be genetic so if they are in your genes, you may inherit it one day without having to experience a tragedy to "trigger" it. It might activate over weeks or months and it may happen so slowly, you don't even realize how much you have changed until years later.

  A mental illness can trigger if you experience a horrific tragedy. As the months go by, the illness might make you enraged or terrified. But you might not see it as an illness. You might think you are childish because you can't get over the past. It can take years to learn that you have a mental illness.

  And it can take just as long to receive the correct treatment or medication.

285. Depressed people look depressed.

Those who suffer clinical depression tend to exude their depression. Many famous clinical depressives over the years were very open about their struggle with depression like Edgar Allen Poe, Sylvia Plath and Virginia Woolf.

However, those who suffer from manic depression seem like the last people you would ever expect to have depression. Manic depressives have moments of high and low. When they have high moments, they seem like the happiest, funniest people in the world. People like this tend to hide their dark moments so most of their close friends and family would never suspect they have this illness.

286. People who are mentally ill can just get "cured."

If you have a phobia or suffer bipolar or experience clinical depression, how do you get rid of it?

Face your demons? Face your past? Face yourself? Find the love of your life? Stop being angry or sad or afraid? Have an epiphany?

The best-case scenario is you will need medication. But normally, the road is long and arduous with a few relapses from time to time.

It's not an accurate idea to magically cure mental illness but to treat it.

Mental illnesses can be treated for years, maybe for the person's entire life, rather than with a snap of your fingers.

287. Mentally ill people are dangerous.

The Appleby study of 2001 confirmed that mentally ill people are more likely to be attacked rather than attack someone else.

The Hiday study of 1999 validated that the mentally ill are 2 ½ times more likely to be attacked or mugged than the general population.

If a mentally ill person has an episode or is experiencing side effects from their medication or lack of, they are prone to anxiety, disorientation, depression, and fear.

They aren't going to start attacking people for no reason. If they suffer an episode in public, they might ask for help from a total stranger, which can freak out some people. Others might attack a mentally ill person, thinking that they are about to be attacked or robbed.

288. If someone is having an epileptic fit, put a book in their mouth to prevent them from biting their tongue.

Everyone has bitten their tongue. It's annoying but not excruciating. You know what is excruciating? Biting down on a book over and over again until it does damage to your jaws and teeth.

Also, epileptics can easily bite someone who comes near their mouths. Different epileptics have different treatments. Some need medication, some need an ambulance and some just need to be held down until the fit is over.

289.   Most NASA workers have dyslexia because a dyslexic mind is better at dealing with the mathematical precision required for the job.

There's this idea that dyslexics are more likely to be hired by NASA because dyslexics are better at calculating 3D patterns, sequential convergences and blah blah blah it's not true. In a nutshell – having dyslexia will not help your chances of getting a job at NASA.

This misconception has become so popular that NASA had to dismiss it on Twitter recently.

290.   If you have a panic attack, breathe into a paper bag.

Breathing into a paper bag in mid-panic attack can make you pass out. People tend to say, "Take a deep breath" but that can cut off blood flow in certain parts of your body, which can paralyze your arms, legs, and face causing you to panic more.

Small, quick breaths are the most effective tactic. Over time, your body will relax and the panic will subside.

MISCELLANEOUS

291.   The best time to book a flight is Monday.
People believe Monday is the best time to book a
flight because that is when flights are announced.
However, by Tuesday, airlines start to match the
sale prices of their competitors and their own
prices will go down.

In the future, book on a Tuesday.

**292.   You need to get twenty-one points to win a
game of table tennis.**
The rules have been changed recently. The game
is now up to eleven.

293.   Opposites attract.
It always appears that way because any
personality difference will stand out in a
relationship e.g. if one person loves animals but
the other person hates animals.

But a 2003 study showed that people are
attracted to fundamental similarities like
socioeconomic class, being interested in
monogamy and children.

**294.   The best time to get the cheapest prices at
Christmas is Black Friday.**
Anyone who's worked in a retail shop will tell
you that many retailers will introduce their most
drastic markdowns two weeks before the holiday
to avoid being overstocked in the New Year.

295.   If you set your thermostat really low, it will cool down faster.

No matter how you set the thermostat, it cools down at a steady level.

296.   When you shop for a diamond, get a full carat.

The average customer won't know much about diamonds so they tend to get one-carat diamonds, unaware that 0.95 carat is three times cheaper. The size difference is completely unnoticeable to the untrained eye.

297.   If you want clean clothes, don't set your washing machine to use cold.

Cold water will prevent your clothes from shrinking or staining (especially from sweat.)

298.   You can use sprinklers to flood an entire building.

We've all seen this in movies like The Matrix or Die Hard where the hero sets off one sprinkler, triggering every sprinkler in the building to go off.

But sprinklers don't work this way. If they did, most businesses would go out of business very quickly due to water damage. Sprinklers aren't linked up. They operate individually. If a fire set off a sprinkler, the other sprinkles won't activate until the fire catches up with them.

Also, sprinklers can't be activated by flipping a switch or pressing a button except in extremely high-security rooms where fire could cause incontrovertible damage.

299. Water at the bottom of your dishwasher means that it is broken.

Thank God I learned this because this happened to me last week and my wife and I nearly wasted money on a new dishwasher!

After a heavy load, this water works as a failsafe to prevent leaks which could lead to your dishwasher actually breaking.

300. Washing dishes by hand saves more money than washing them in a dishwasher.

This may have been true a few decades ago but modern dishwashers waste far less water so it's more sensible just to put your dirty dishes in the dishwasher.

301. You should put knives in the dishwasher.

Knives should be cleaned by hand. The shaking of the dishwasher will eventually dull your knives.

302. Subliminal messages in advertising are effective.

The cult classic film, They Live, popularized this idea. In the movie, a man (played by the recently deceased Roddy Piper) finds a special pair of glasses that allows him to see that every billboard on Earth has secret messages like "Conform," "Obey" or "Consume" which is why people live drone-like lives. The idea of subliminal messages originates from James Vicary who discussed his theory in 1957. However, he eventually admitted that there was no proof that subliminal messages work. The idea hasn't been taken seriously since.

303. You can smother a person with a pillow.
When someone is smothered with a pillow in movies like One Flew Over the Cuckoo's Nest, it only takes about forty seconds.

In reality, it would take up to five minutes. Also, if someone was smothering you with a pillow, you could just... turn your head. Problem solved.

The only cases in reality where people have been smothered by pillows are when the victims were unconscious or very old.

304. You don't need to wash your coffeemaker.
Some people never clean their coffeemaker. Not only should you clean it but you should clean it every single day you use it.

Why? Mold. The more often you clean your coffeemaker, the less mold will build up.

305. You can't fold a piece of paper in half more than seven times.
A US high school student called Britney Gallivan folded a piece of paper twelve times.

306. Therapy involves discussing your dreams.
If you have never seen a therapist, you may believe that talking about dreams is a big factor. Even the very first episode of The Sopranos plays with this idea when the main character visits his therapist.

However, most neuropsychologists find oneiric analysis (the study of dreams) unnecessary, unhelpful and even pointless.

307. Breaking glass is easy.

In action movies, actors effortlessly smash glass like it's made of Papier Machet. Schwarzenegger or Stallone shatter glass in their movies just by looking at it.

But glass is sturdier than you might think. There are many videos on YouTube of carjackers trying to break into vehicles with bricks and hammers but they underestimated the strength of the glass. And there is another misconception people make about glass.

308. Breaking glass isn't dangerous.

You might think, "Ok, I know when glass breaks in a movie, it's just a movie. But I know in real life, glass can be really dangerous!"

And that's true. In reality, you couldn't get up after being smashed through glass. You would be shredded by shards of glass, which can be fatal.

But would you believe that safety glass is dangerous? Safety glass is used on glass shower doors. Although this is the "safe" type of glass, window expert, Mark Meshulam, says that hundreds of people are sent to the emergency room every year when this safety glass shatters.

309. Embalming a body means that the organs have to be removed.

That's an autopsy. It's true that Ancient Egyptians removed organs from their dead during their embalming process but things have come a long way nowadays. All an embalmer needs now is to access an artery with an one-inch incision.

310. Biker gangs are criminals.

The idea that biker gangs are gangsters is easy to believe thanks to the show, Sons of Anarchy and the recent biker gang shootout in Texas that left nine dead.

According to a sergeant on the scene, it was the worst crime he had scene in thirty years. Because of this, it's going to taint all of the good that biker gangs have done over the last twenty years. The main thing that biker gangs represent is the fight against child abuse. Bikers Against Child Abuse is a volunteer group in thirty-six states since 1995. Bikers will protect children being bullied, assaulted or abused and even walk them to court or parole hearings against their potential attackers.

311. In the US, you get an automatic 4.0 if your college roommate commits suicide.

This idea comes from the movies, Dead Man's Curve and Dead Man on Campus (both of which came out in 1998, have the same story, nearly have the same title and they are both equally terrible.)

This is simply an urban legend.

<u>MUSIC</u>

312.   Bruce Springsteen has had a No. 1 hit.
Bruce has sold 120 million records, won twenty
Grammys, two Golden Globes, and an Academy
Award. "Born in the USA" and "Born to Run" are
the two best-selling albums in American music
history. In spite of all of his success, he's never
had a No. 1 hit.

313.   Nirvana has had a No. 1 hit.
Although Nirvana changed grunge music forever,
they only released three albums before lead
singer, Kurt Cobain's death. None of their songs
reached No. 1.

314.   Led Zeppelin have had a No. 1 hit.
Led Zeppelin are the sixth-best selling artists
ever (behind The Beatles, Elvis, Michael Jackson,
Madonna and Elton John). They are often
considered to be the creators of heavy metal.
Even thought Stairway to Heaven is the most
requested song in American radio history, they
have never had a No. 1 hit.

315.   Bob Dylan has a No. 1 hit.
Bob Dylan has never had a No. 1 hit. But Justin
Bieber has. There are so many things wrong with
the world.

316.   The Who have had a No. 1 hit.
Nope. This is ridiculous! Who's next? Bob Marley?

317. Bob Marley has had a No. 1 hit.

 Not even close. The most successful song he sang was Roots, Rock, Reggae which climbed No. 51 in the charts.

And if you think this couldn't be more insulting...

318. Jimi Hendrix has had a No. 1 hit.

I don't even want to write the details about this one. It's too depressing. Jimi had three albums before he suddenly died at 27. His albums never even came close to No. 1.

PEOPLE

319. **Donald Trump is a self-made billionaire.**
     He got a little help from his father, Fred Trump who already had 300 million dollars. Trump has been bankrupt three times and has only been bailed out by his inheritance.

320. **Women speak way more than men.**
     A study in Arizona State University declared that men and women speak the same amount of words per day – 16,000.

321. **Therapists are cool, calm, and collected professionals with perfectly balance minds.**
     If you needed counselling because you felt mentally imbalanced, it's safe to assume that the therapist who is helping you must be extremely mentally balanced.

     However, because therapists have to deal with dozens of unstable people per week, each suffering from phobias, mental illness, depression, self-harm or suicidal tendencies, it's not uncommon for the job to take its toll on a therapist's mind. Many therapists see other therapists. Even Sigmund Freud said this was a good idea to keep therapists "in check."

322. **Alfred Hitchcock won an Oscar for Best Picture.**
     Hitch never won Best Picture for any of his films.

323. Alfred Hitchcock was a horror film director.
In fifty-four years, Hitchcock made over fifty films.

Only two of his famous movies are horror films. He is known for directing horror because his slasher film, Psycho is considered to be arguably his greatest movie. While Hitchcock was often in the public eye, he followed Psycho up with another horror movie, The Birds.

However many of his classic films like Vertigo, Strangers on a Train, Rear Window, Dial M for Murder, and North by Northwest are more like psychological thrillers rather than horror movies.

324. Arnold Schwarzenegger became a millionaire when he turned into an action star.
It's easy to assume Arnold was a big dumb jock who owes all of his success to luckily falling into Hollywood.

But Arnie was very successful before he became a movie star. He was already a millionaire before his very first movie.

And it wasn't from bodybuilding as you might assume but from bricklaying. He advertised himself as a specialty European bricklayer to sound more like a powerhouse company. It worked, as he became a millionaire within a year of moving in the States at only twenty-one years of age.

325.   Peter O' Toole has won an Oscar for Best Actor.

He won an Honorary Academy Award at the end of his life but... come on. They don't count. That's just the Academy's way of saying, "Sorry you didn't win when you deserved to a few decades ago."

326.   Donald Sutherland has won an Oscar.

Although he is now more well known as the villain in The Hunger Games series, Sutherland has been acting for over half a century so it's safe to assume that he won an Oscar for... something. But he didn't.

327.   Gary Oldman has won an Oscar for Best Actor.

You know what's worse than Gary Oldman never winning an Oscar?

Cher has won one. Seriously.

328.   Ridley Scott has won an Oscar for Best Director.

I could give a hundred examples of movies, directors, and actors whom you would assume have won an Oscar but they haven't.

But Ridley Scott didn't win one?!?! The guy who made Alien and Blade Runner? What's wrong with the world?

329.   The Disney logo is Walt Disney's signature.

It isn't. It's just a logo. Looks pretty though.

330. **Walt Disney is cryogenically frozen.**

This is a conspiracy theory more than anything but I have to include it because I have heard it so many times over the past decade.

Walt was obsessed with the idea of cryogenesis. However, he was cremated when he died in 1966 from lung cancer.

331. **Walt Disney created Mickey Mouse.**

Mickey Mouse was created by Ub Iwerks. Although he is considered a co-creator, Walt stated that Ub created the famous Disney character. Ub even animated Mickey Mouse's first official cartoon, Steamboat Willie.

He was forgotten because he was simply too shy to promote himself.

332. **There is a picture of Uncle Ben on the front of Uncle Ben's rice.**

Gordon Harwell was in charge of a rice business in the 1950s. When he decided to expand his company, he wanted a mascot and a catchy name.

He saw an elderly black gentleman called Frank Brown in a restaurant he often visited and thought he had a good face to help sell his rice.

Harwell knew of a successful black rice farmer living in Texas who called himself Uncle Ben. He liked the sound of "Uncle Ben" and Ben had a great reputation so Harwell thought Ben's name and Frank's face would sell his product.

333. Batman was created by Bob Kane.

Kane is always credited with creating the most beloved superhero (sorry Superman, you had your day.) Even today, Kane's name is on Batman films, movies, and comic books.

But he never created Batman. Kane's partner, Bill Finger created the dark superhero. Finger invented Batman's tragic backstory, his villains, the city of Gotham, the costume, Commissioner Gordon, the Batmobile, Robin, the idea of having a superhero with no powers, his gadgets and his nickname, The Dark Knight. Kane was considering calling him Birdman (which is weird because Michael Keaton has played both.)

The only part of Batman that Kane created was that the Bat-suit had wings. That's it. The suit itself was red until Finger made it dark (and awesome.)

Because Finger was such a bad businessman, he never profited from his creations and Kane hogged all the credit for decades.

Finger died in poverty and most of the world's biggest Batman fans have never heard of him.

334. Steven Spielberg got his first job at Universal Studios by showing up with a suit and briefcase, finding an empty office and pretending he worked there.

It's a lovely story but it's not true. Spielberg's uncle got him the job at Universal Studios because he already worked there.

335. Bruce Lee died from an allergic reaction to aspirin.

Many people inaccurately believe that Bruce Lee died because he was allergic to aspirin. The drug he took is called Equagesic (which is an aspirin.) However, he was allergic to meprobamate, an ingredient in that type of aspirin. I may sound like I am splitting hairs but this sort of misunderstanding is exactly what led to Lee's death. He knew he had no problems with aspirin and had taken anti-inflammatory medication many times as he recovered from injuries during his fighting scenes. But he had never taken Equagesic before and was oblivious to the fact that one of its ingredients was lethal for him.

336. Psychiatrists and psychologists are the same thing.

These terms are often used interchangeably but they are two very different professions. Psychiatrists prescribe drugs and psychologists don't.

337. JK Rowling was a poverty-stricken single parent when she wrote Harry Potter.

Rowling's difficult life has been heavily exaggerated to make it sound more tragic. To quote JK Rowling herself, "I was working full time as I did for my entire adult life, and I was not a single parent. I finished the book under those conditions. But it obviously does make a better story. It sounds more like a rags-to-riches tale."

PHYSICAL HEALTH

338. **You can only get appendicitis once.**
An Englishman called David Beminster is one of the rare examples of a person who suffered from appendicitis twice. He had his appendix removed in a hospital in Surrey in 2007. In 2008, he started suffering intense pains in his abdomen. When he described the symptoms to doctors, they said it sounded like appendicitis. When he assured him it was removed, they dismissed it and assumed it must be a tummy bug.

Eventually, he went to hospital and learned that a small amount of his appendix was still in his abdomen and it had become inflamed. He learned that during appendix removal, it is common for surgeons to leave a tiny part of the appendix within the abdomen, as it is very painful and dangerous to remove. It should only be removed when absolutely necessary. Unfortunately, David had to be that rare example.

339. **You can only have your tonsils removed once.**
Tonsil surgery has the same paradox as appendix surgery. When a patient has his tonsils removed, only 80% of the tonsils are eliminated. Removing them in their entirety is more difficult and excruciating. The chance of the tonsils growing back is very slim but it is possible which means that they can becomes inflamed once more and have to be removed again.

340. When you get a kidney transplant, surgeons remove your old kidneys.

When you get new kidneys, your old kidneys are usually left in your body. There is actually a surprising amount of space in the area near your kidneys. Removing the kidneys is more dangerous than leaving them in. They don't get removed unless they become infected.

341. You should put hydrogen peroxide on an infected wound.

Most houses have a bottle of hydrogen peroxide lying around somewhere, which is supposed to be used on wounds to prevent the spread of infection. When you pour hydrogen peroxide on a wound, it reacts by foaming up. It looks cool but it doesn't help the wound at all. Antibiotic creams like Neosporin are effective on wounds. If you are out of antibiotics, Vaseline is a good substitute.

342. Diabetes is caused by sugar.

High blood sugar is a symptom of diabetes, not a cause.

Your pancreas produces insulin, which delivers sugar to your cells. If you eat too much of anything (whether it's fatty food or fruit,) you can exhaust your pancreas so it can no longer produce enough insulin to function.

But that's only Type 2 diabetes.

Type 1 diabetes tends to happen in childhood and is caused by genetics rather than your sugar intake.

343. People who suffer from gigantism are always tall.

There are two main types of gigantism. Both forms originate from a tumor in the pituitary gland in the brain. This tumor produces an excess of growth hormone, which causes the person's size to rapidly increase.

If a person develops the tumor before they reach the end of puberty, they become extremely tall (7 or 8ft tall.) This is called acromegalic gigantism.

If a person develops the tumor after puberty, they tend to grow outwardly and have a very wide appearance. They may only be a bit tall (6ft 3) but they may an overly large head and they may have a size 20 shoe. This type of gigantism is simply called acromegaly.

344. The best way to determine food allergies is with a blood test.

At least 50% of blood tests will give a false positive with food allergies.

The most effective way is to do the Oral Food Challenge. The allergist will give you small doses of food that you suspect you are allergic to. If there is a small reaction, then they can confirm your allergies.

345. Allergies are for life.

Almost all children have allergies (especially with food) but most allergies are outgrown by the time children are ten years old.

346. You may be allergic to penicillin.

Many people believe they are allergic to penicillin because they had a reaction to it when they were young. But a lot of allergies wear off when children grow up. If you had an allergy to penicillin as a child, there is a 90% chance that it has faded.

I'm not saying it is impossible for adults not to be allergic to penicillin (my wife is.) But if you're not sure, you should check. It could be the difference between life and death.

347. You can't do a CT scan if you are allergic to shellfish.

Before a CT scan, a patient needs to absorb an iodonic dye. Shellfish also have iodine, which is where the idea comes from that people with this allergy can't have CT scans. However, people who are allergic to shellfish aren't allergic to iodine. They are allergic to shellfish protein.

348. If you get cancer when you are young, you have a better chance of surviving.

There is no ideal fighting-age for cancer. Cancer isn't a disease. It's your own cells attacking you. The younger you are, the faster you grow. The faster you grow, the faster your cells produce and travel and the faster cancer can spread. Children or teenagers can be ravaged with cancer within a few weeks. It's far slower for the elderly. Prolific actor, Ian McKellen was diagnosed with prostate cancer in 2009. But since McKellen is in his seventies, the cancer moves so slowly that it has very little effect on his life.

349. Cancer hurts.
Cancer rarely hurts and when it does, it's usually too late to do anything about it. Most of the pain a cancer sufferer will experience will be from the treatment and medication rather than the cancer itself.

350. Drug addicts can't function in real life.
There are some addicts who are so consumed by their addiction that they will blow all their money on heroin.

But there are other addicts known as functioning addicts who need to maintain their addiction so badly, that they find a balance in their lives because they want to keep their addictions stimulated in the long run. This means that they could have consistent jobs, friends, stable relationship and children.

They can keep this up for years, sometimes decades. You would be astonished at who these functioning addicts may be. They could be the last person you would ever suspect.

351. Drug addicts and dealers look like they are involved in drugs.
Drug addicts and dealers will do everything in their power to not look like they are involved in drugs. Drug dealers aren't necessarily sleazy, vicious, alpha-male gangsters. Sadly, in this day and age, people as young as teenagers can

become drug dealers They won't do this for obvious reasons like poverty or desperation. It can be for reasons as petty as popularity, peer pressure, boredom or extra cash.

352. **Meth-addicts look scrawny and scabby.**
This can happen but society tends to believe that this is what ALL meth-addicts look like because they use it as a scare tactic to show the damage methamphetamines can cause.

PLACES

353. **Holland is another word for the Netherlands.**
The kingdom of The Netherlands has only existed since 1830. Nowadays, The Netherlands is composed of twelve counties including North Holland and South Holland. The major cities of The Netherlands are located in the Hollands (Amsterdam, Rotterdam and The Hague) so if you have visited The Netherlands or know somebody from there, it's likely they are from Holland.

Before 1830, many trading ships would travel from the Hollands to all other regions in Europe. The traders were known to be from Holland so when the twelve provinces were formed, Europeans were still dealing with the same Holland traders that were now saying they were from The Netherlands. Naturally, people assumed that Holland and The Netherlands were one and the same.

If you ever visit The Netherlands, please don't make that mistake. It is considered rude.

354. **Nigeria has a prince.**
If you check your email, you will, at some point in your life, have received spam saying that you will receive money if you give them your credit card details. The most famous example of this is an email from a Nigerian prince who will give you a fortune if you give him your bank details. This story is not only baloney but it is impossible since Nigeria doesn't even have a prince!

355. Birth rates in the U.S. are out of control.
American birthrates are at their lowest since they started tracking them in the 1950s.

During the 50s, there were 118 births per 1,000 women of childbearing age per year. In 2013, there were 63 per 1,000.

356. Teen pregnancy rates are crazier than ever.
Teen pregnancy has dropped by half since the 1950s. In 1957, there were an average of 96 births per 1,000 women aged 15-19 in the U.S.. By the year 2000, that number plummeted to 49.

This is a record low for American teens in this age group, and a drop of 6% from 2011. So it's not just going down over the last few decades but every year.

Birth rates fell 8% for women aged 15-17 years old, and 5% for women aged 18-19 years old.

In 2012, a total of 205,388 babies were born to women aged 15-19 years for a live birth rate of 29.4 per 1,000 women in this age group.

Not only are more American teens using contraception, more of them are abstaining from sex until they are older.

357. Dropping high school in the U.S. has never been higher.
Since the 1970s, the high school dropout rate has been cut in half. The dropout rate in 1970 was 14.6%.

In 2014, the rate was 7.1%

358.   In modern society, people are getting married way too young.

The number of young adults getting married has halved since the 1960s. The number of 18-31 year olds living with a spouse in 1968 was 56%. In 2012, it was 23%

359.   College students are lazy.

College students are considered privileged compared to our parents time. However, twice as many students have jobs today compared to thirty years ago. Between 55% of students now work full-time or part-time. It was less than half that in 1984.

360.   Drug use in teenagers is getting worse every year.

Teenage drug use has been steadily declining over the last twenty years. 27% of American eighth, tenth and twelfth graders have been reported for using illicit drugs in 2014.

In 1997, it was 34%.

Availability and consumption of alcohol, cigarettes, marijuana, powder cocaine, crystal methamphetamine, and prescription painkillers are also on the decline.

361.   Smoking in America is on the rise.

Smoking has halved since the 1950s. In 1954, 45% of Americans smoked cigarettes. In 2014, that number was 21%.

35% of people smoked a pack a day in 1954.

20% of people smoked a pack a day in 2014.

362. People are dying younger than ever.
There are ten times as many people over 65 today as there were a century ago. In 1900, there were 3.1 million Americans over 65.
In 2000, there was 35 million.

363. People are watching T.V. more than ever.
T.V. viewing has dropped 27% among young adults in the last four years. Between the first quarter of 2011 and the fourth quarter of 2014, television viewing by Americans who were 18-24 years old decreased by 27%.

364. Poverty worldwide has skyrocketed.
I in 2 people lived in extreme poverty in 1950.
1 in 5 people lived in extreme poverty in 2005.
Studies have shown that 1 in 40 people will live in extreme poverty by 2050.

365. Poverty in poor countries is worse than ever.
Since 1990, the number of people in developing countries living in extreme poverty has halved. The number dropped from 43% to 21% between 1990 and 2010, a reduction of nearly a billion people.

366. U.S. taxes are higher than ever.
Taxes in America are lower than ¾ of the other countries in the world. The average single American is paying an average of about 25% of their paycheck for income tax and social safety taxes, which is well below the Organization for

Economic Cooperation and Development (OECD) average of just under 36%.

367. Colombia is a haven for cocaine.
The annual rate of cocaine production in Colombia is 0.7%. That's lower than America. That's lower than Canada! Who knew Canada was such a dark horse? Peru is the largest source of cocaine.

368. Marijuana is a huge problem in The Netherlands.
It's only legal to sell five grams of pot in The Netherlands. You are legally allowed to possess far more in Costa Rica, Czech Republic, Ecuador, Norway, Peru. France, Italy, America and Canada. (Canada is like a secret rebel for drugs.) These countries inhale far more marijuana than The Netherlands.

369. Madagascar is a tropical rain forest.
The movie, Madagascar, has popularized this idea. Most of the rain forest is on the east coast of Madagascar. Saying that Madagascar is "just a rainforest" is like saying Ireland is heavily mountainous just because there are some mountains in it. Madagascar is a mix of desert, grassland, dry forests, farms and rainforest.

370. The Galapagos Islands are full of wildlife.
The Galapagos Islands are where Charles Darwin molded his theory of evolution. Because of this, it's easy to assume the Galapagos is filled with

tropical wildlife. In actual fact, the Galapagos is filled with volcanoes and desert and is overpopulated by human life.

371. Texas is mostly desert.
Most non-Americans will assume that Texas is mainly deserts thanks to cowboy movies. Texas has an even amount of different terrains – forest, desert, beaches, canyons, and mountains.

372. Hawaii is a tropical paradise.
Hawaii does have beautiful beaches but not as many as you'd think. The government emphasize the palm tress and sunshine to boost tourism but there's a massive desert in Hawaii as well called Ka'u. Well, technically it's not a desert because it was formed by a volcano. It's more like a charred, smoldered, lifeless terrain. Not the image you would picture when you think of Hawaii, is it?

373. The Great Wall of China looks like how it appears in photographs.
I've been to the Great Wall. Twice. I can tell you from personal experience that over 99% of it is in ruins. Any photographs you have seen of the Wall are from Beijing where some of the Wall has been restored.

374. The Great Wall of China is in China.
The Wall is 13,170 miles long. It's so long that it covers three countries – China, North Korea and Mongolia.

375. **The Hanging Gardens of Babylon is one of the Seven Wonders of the Ancient World.**
Babylon has no records of these Gardens. Historians believe that soldiers returning to Greece from Babylon exaggerated what they saw. The Gardens were pretty at best; not so awesome that they deserve to be put in the same bracket as The Great Wall of China or The Pyramid of Giza.

376. **Deserts are mostly made up of sand.**
20% of the world's deserts are made up of sand. Most deserts are composed of rock, salt, shingle and even snow.

<u>PRONUNCIATIONS</u>

377. **Beijing is pronounced "Bay-zhhing."**
China's capital is pronounced "Bey-Jing."

378. **Iraq is pronounced "EYE-rack."**
I always say this word incorrectly. It's "ee-ROCK."

379. **Dubai is pronounced "Doo-BYE."**
It's Du-BAY."

380. **Reykjavik is pronounced "RAKE-ja-vik."**
Iceland's capital is pronounced "REY-kya-vik."
(And it's a lovely place.)

381. **Hiroshima is pronounced Hir-rosh-im-ma."**
Considering Hiroshima suffered the worst attack in history, you'd think the least we could do is pronounce the name of the city correctly. It's pronounced "Hir-row-sheem-ma."

382. **Pakistan is pronounced "PAK-uh-Stan."**
It's pronounced "PAH-kee-Stahn" in spite of the fact I have never heard a single person ever say it that way.

383. **Qatar is pronounced "Kwa-tar."**
Not even close. This country is pronounced "Kuh-Ter."

384. **Budapest is pronounced "Boo-da-PEST."**
It's "Boo-da-PESHT."

385. **Bangkok is pronounced "BANG-kok."**
It's "Bahng-Gawk."

386. **Versailles is pronounced "Ver-SAYLZ."**
It's "Ver-SYE."

387. **Ralph Fiennes' name is pronounced "Ralph Fines."**
The actor who played Voldermort in the Harry Potter series often has his name mispronounced. His first name is pronounced "Rafe."

388. **The director Martin Scorcese's name is pronounced "Martin Score-sez-ay."**
The director of Raging Bull and Goodfellas often has his surnamed mispronounced. It's pronounced "Score-sez-see."

389. **Steve Buscemi's name is pronounced "Steve Boo-shem-me."**
Steve says he pronounces it "Boo-semi" but he does point out that the correct way to pronounce the name in its country of origin (Italy) is "Boo-shame-me." So everybody pronounces it wrong. Including him.

390. **Kirsten Dunst's name is pronounced "Kirsten Dunst."**
This actress famously played Mary-Jane Watson in the Spider-Man movies (the good ones.) But her name is pronounced "Keers-tin Dunst."

391. Rihanna's name is pronounced "Ree-awn-ah."
It's "Ree-ahnne-uh." Even her husband has gotten this wrong.

392. Amanda Seyfried's name is pronounced "Amanda Say-fried."
This actress has become big from Mean Girls many years ago yet no one has learned to say her name correctly. Her surname is pronounced "Sigh-frid."

393. Charlize Theron's name is pronounced "Charleez Thir-rone."
She won an Oscar for Monster, was awesome in Mad Max Fury Road and people still can't say her name. It's pronounced "Shar-leez Ther-un."

394. Joaquin Phoenix's name is pronounced "Joe-a-kwin Phoenix."
He made his career playing the villain in Gladiator yet people struggle pronouncing his name fifteen years later. His name is pronounced like "Wa-keen Phoenix."

395. Shia LeBeouf's name is pronounced "Shy Li-Bay-of."
The star from the Transformers franchise has a tricky name. It's pronounced "Shy-ya Le-Buff."

396. Saoirse Ronan's name is pronounced "Say-orsh-she Ro-nan."
Although she is famous for Atonement, Anna Karenina, Hanna, and The Host, few people

outside of Ireland can pronounce her name. Saorise's name is Gaelic so you can't pronounce it the way it looks. It's pronounced "Seer-shu Row-nin."

397. Milla Jovovich's name is pronounced "Mil-la Jo-vo-vitch."

This Ukrainian actress became famous after playing Leelu in The Fifth Element. But the correct way to pronounce her name is "Mee-luh Yo-vo-vitch." It even says so on her Twitter account.

<u>QUOTES</u>

398. **In Jaws, Rob Scheider's character says, "We're gonna need a bigger boat."**

He actually says, "You're gonna need a bigger boat." This sounds like a pedantic correction but this comes up in a lot of pub quizzes.

399. **Philip Sheridan said, "The only good Indian is a dead Indian."**

He said, "The only good Indians I ever saw were dead." He meant that he had seen great heroes who died in battle but his quote was taken out of context to make it sound like he hated Indians.

400. **In the film, Apocalypse Now, Colonel Kilgore says the famous quote, "I love the smell of napalm in the morning. Smells like victory."**

The exact quote is, "I love the smell of napalm in the morning. You know, one time we had a hill bombed, for twelve hours. When it was all over, I walked up. We didn't find one of 'em, not one stinkin' dink body. The smell, you know that gasoline smell, the whole hill. Smelled like… victory."

401. **Voltaire said, "I disapprove of what you say, but I will defend to the death your right to say it."**

That's the best sentence ever. Too bad he didn't say it.

402. **Marie Antoinette said, "Let them eat cake" to starving peasants.**

I'll assume this is in the movie but it never happened in real life.

403. **"He's Alive!" is a line from Frankenstein.**
The line is, "It's alive."

404. **Sigmund Freud said, "Sometimes a cigar is just a cigar."**

He never said this.

405. **Mark Twain coined the phrase, "The only two certainties in life are death and taxes."**

Twain was the first famous person to say this phrase. But Christopher Bullock was the first to say, "T'is impossible to be sure of anything but Death and Taxes in his work, Cobler of Preston.

406. **"No computer will need more than 640 kilobytes" was an incredibly inaccurate statement made by Bill Gates.**

Bill Gates has many times admitted to inaccurate predictions he has made but he never said this.

407. **"Everything that can be invented, has been invented" was said by Charles Duell just before the invention of cars, television, planes, computers, and spaceships.**

This would be the most inaccurate quote ever but Duell, the Commissioner of U.S. Patents never said it. In fact, he believed the exact opposite.

<u>RELIGION</u>

408. The most powerful being in Ancient Greek mythology was Zeus.

No, and just in case you thought you were sneaky, it wasn't his father, Cronus either.

The most powerful being in Greece's mythology was the Hekatonkheires.

There were three of these creatures called Briareos, Cottus and Gyges. They were insurmountably powerful because they had one hundred arms and fifty heads (some writings say they had a hundred heads.)

They were the children of Gaia who herself was created at the beginning of the universe in Greece's mythology.

For such a powerful fascinating creature, the Hekatonkheires isn't as well known as the other Greek gods (unless you played God of War.) These beings are not mentioned often but they are known to have "a strength and ferocity that surpassed all of the gods."

409. Wicca is an ancient religion.

Your grandparents are probably older than Wicca.

Gerald Gardner invented Wicca in 1954. Wiccans get mixed up with druids because they have similarities such as hooded robes, spiritual fulfillment, totems, and... wait...

410. **We know a lot about the ancient Druids.**
We know next to nothing about druidism.
Although what historians have known about
Druids is often depicted in stories as an ancient
religion that believed in sacrifices and spells and
incantations, we have no evidence what they
believed because they left no historical records.
We only know ancient Druids existed because the
Romans and Greeks mention them several times
in their records.

The idea that Druids were into magic comes
from Neo-Druidism, a Welsh sect in 1792. It was
formed by Edward Williams who called himself
Iolo Morgannwg (because it sounded Druidy) but
it is clear he made this religion up for money and
copied all of its "beliefs" from other religions.

411. **"It is more likely a camel can enter the eye of a
needle than a rich man to enter the kingdom of
heaven" is a misunderstanding. The Needle is a
thin gate in Israel that is too skinny for a camel to
enter.**
That quote literally means a rich man can't enter
heaven. There is no Needle gate. Rich men didn't
like the idea that they were barred from God's
kingdom so they concocted the notion of a Needle
gate.

412. **"God works in mysterious ways" is a quote in
the Bible.**
This quote stems from William Cowper's hymn of
the same name, which was written in 1773.

413. An upside-down crucifix is a Satanist symbol.
If a cross is a symbol of Jesus, surely an inverted cross is a symbol of Satan, right?

No.

The first Pope, Saint Peter, was crucified upside down because he didn't feel worthy to be crucified the same way as Christ. This symbol is used by the Catholic Church to commemorate their first Pope. You can see this symbol on the current Pope's throne.

So when Satanists (and most heavy metal bands) use the inverted cross to be cool or whatever, they are actually saying that they respect St. Peter.

414. The Behemoth was a fictional monster in the Bible.
The Behemoth is described as "hidden among the reeds in the marsh," "the stream surrounds it," "power in the muscles of its belly," and "its tail sways like a cedar. Recent scholars believe that "cedar" description is a mistranslation and are now firm it is meant to mean "cedar branch." If this is true, the description perfectly describes one creature on Earth – a hippo.

415. It took Noah several years to build the Ark.
According to the Bible, Noah was 600 years old when he started building the Ark and he finished it when he was 720.

It took Noah 120 years to build the Ark. That must've been really boring.

416. Jesus condemns homosexuality in the Bible.
Jesus never mentions homosexuality in the Bible.
It is Paul that condemns it.

417. The most common name in the Bible is Christ.
Christ is mentioned in the Bible 973 times.
> But David is mentioned 1,011 times.
> "Simon" is the most common name in the
Bible.

418. God destroyed Sodom and Gomorrah for homosexuality.
> Sodom and Gomorrah were destroyed for their
> wicked ways. There is no reference to
> homosexuality throughout this story.

419. There are seven circles of Hell mentioned in the Bible.
> This reference comes from Dante's Inferno, not
> the Bible.

420. The seven deadly sins are in the Bible.
> The seven deadly sins have been popularized by
> the movie Se7en (which is still a really dumb title
> for such a good movie) but they are never
> mentioned in the Bible. The idea that Gluttony,
> Greed, Sloth, Lust, Pride, Envy, Wrath are the
> seven deadly sins originated in medieval times so
> society knew what the Church forbade.
> You might wonder why people of the time
> didn't simply read the Bible to learn what the
> Church allowed and disallowed. Which brings me
> to my next point.

**421. People have always known what was written
in the Bible.**

The way we know the Bible today didn't exist for
over a millennium after it was written. It was
originally written on scrolls and parchments
rather than a book.

Society only had their own bibles in the last
few hundred years. Before that, people outside of
the Catholic Church had very little understanding
of what was written in the Bible. Even if the
common people got a copy, the scriptures were
written in Latin, which no one could read outside
of the Church. So for a long time, Europeans'
knowledge of God came directly from priests. It
was only when the printing press became
popularized and Martin Luther translated the
Bible into German that people finally got to read
the Bible themselves. Luther assumed this would
end debates about religion. In case you haven't
been on the Internet ever, that is still a problem.

422. Purgatory is mentioned in the Bible.

The idea of purgatory didn't exist until the
Council of Florence devised it in 1431. The Bible
said that only the pure go to Heaven and the
wicked are banished to Hell. But what about the
inbetweeny people? What about a good person
who occasionally commits small sins? What
about the good people who died before Christ
was born? What about a baby that died before it
had a chance to be baptized? Do innocent babies
deserve to go to Hell? (Who would've ever
thought the Bible would be confusing?)

The Council decided that there must be a place after death where decent souls go to be purified before ascending to Heaven. This became known as Purgatory. Unbaptized babies soul were said to go to a limbo. (What do they do there? Float around forever?)

423.   Jesus sat with his disciples for his final meal as is depicted in Da Vinci's painting, The Last Supper.

Jesus and his disciples crouched before a one-foot tall table for their final supper together as was common practice at the time. They didn't sit on chairs.

424.   Jesus's life story is copied from other religions.

In the documentary, Religulous, Bill Maher explains how Jesus's life is suspiciously similar to the Egyptian god, Horus and the Persian god, Mithras.

Maher states that Horus was born from a virgin, had twelve disciples, was baptized in a river, walked on water, cured the sick and blind, was tempted in the desert, raised Asar from the dead (who's name translates into Lazarus) and he was crucified and resurrected three days later.

Maher also explains how the Persian god, Mithras (who predates Christ by six centuries) was born on December 25th, performed miracles, was known as The Way, The Lamb, The Light, The Messiah, The Savior, and he died and was resurrected three days later.

So not only does Christ's life sound like a remake but it's more of a crossover... like the Avengers movie.

When Christians dismiss the idea that Christ's life just steals elements from other beliefs, it's easy to assume they are being defensive because it shows huge inconsistencies in the foundation of Christianity.

However, Ida B. Pratt and M.L. Bierbrier are adamant that this theory is utterly wrong. And they are not just defensive Christians trying to protect their religion. They are Ancient Egyptologists. First off, Egyptians didn't believe in baptism. Asar doesn't translate into Lazarus. Ancient Egyptians didn't believe any humans had divine powers, not even the Pharaohs.

Also, the idea that Christ had similarities to Mithras comes from a documentary called Zeitgeist, which doesn't cite ANY sources so this concept can't be taken seriously by historians.

TECHNOLOGY

425. Wrapping your head in tinfoil doesn't interfere with satellites.

This idea has become popular again thanks to the HBO show, Better Call Saul.

This theory sounds absurd. The "wrapping your head with tinfoil" concept originated in a 1927 short story by Julian Huxley called The Tissue-Culture King. In this story, the "caps of metal foil" prevented the main character from being mind-controlled.

Now that I've explained where this idea comes from, it seems even more likely that it's utter nonsense. But it isn't. MIT studies confirm that tinfoil hats genuinely reduce the intensity of radio frequency radiation, therefore creating an electromagnetic shield making the person almost invisible to satellite technology.

However, the most effective tool to reduce radio waves is not a tinfoil hat but a wire mesh (such as the one on your tea strainer in the kitchen.) However, wearing one of these on your head would look stupid. But not a tinfoil hat. That looks fine.

426. North Korea hacked Sony in 2014.

Although the exact culprit has yet to be found, almost every cyber expert irrefutably surmised that North Korea didn't have the technological ability to hack SONY and almost all signs point to an inside job.

427.   Most Internet users are American.

One word. China. It's always China.

428.   Airplanes are quick to start.

There are countless movies where someone has to start a plane immediately. To do this, they flip a few switches, push a few buttons, turn some knobs, pull a lever and they're in the air.

We really need to stop getting our facts from movies. Do you know how many checks you need to perform before starting a plane?

79.

And I don't mean you have to do 79 steps before the plane starts. I mean you have to carry out 79 steps before you turn on the plane's engine! Then there are another 44 steps before you take off. So a plane won't be taking off until at least 123 checks are carried out.

429.   In emergencies, airplane cockpits become chaotic.

Blame this misconception on the movies. When there's an aircraft emergency in a movie, the cockpit goes insane with pilots screaming, flashing lights, blaring sirens, etc. If a pilot had to maintain the survival of every passenger on board, he would rely on his years of training and would not want sirens and lights distracting him. In emergencies, the cockpit doesn't become an insane drama. The pilots just act calmly and professionally and deal with the problem as best they can. Working everybody into a frenzy would just make an emergency worse.

430. You can't use electronics on a plane, as it will interfere with the plane's electronics.

Your phone, computer or iPad could never interfere with the electronics of a plane.

This idea is more to do with reassuring bad flyers who are terrified that the plane will crash if there is any electronic interference.

Even though there can be serious fines for using electronic equipment on a plane, it's harmless.

431. If you turn off electronic equipment in your house, they won't use up energy.

Comedian, Michael McIntyre, has a famous sketch about how when people leave the house to go on holiday, they turn off televisions and computers "but not the fridge, we trust the fridge."

However, turning off electronics does not reduce your electricity bills as much as you would imagine because of standby power. 5-10% of electric power is wasted on standby power. If you want to reduce power, you need to unplug plugs, not just switch them off.

432. Car crashes are more frequent than ever.

Since 1921, fatal car crashes have dropped by 95%.

Deaths per million miles driven in 1921 – 24. In 2012, it was 1.13.

433. Nobody uses Yahoo anymore.

I do. So there. Yahoo is the fourth most popular website after Google, Facebook, and YouTube.

434.   If a person was trying to rob you at an ATM, you can alert the police by putting your PIN in the ATM in reverse.

> If this was true, surely banks would have to tell you this when you got a new card. Also, if this was common knowledge, then robbers would know it too so they would know what you would do. On top of that, unless the police can get there in five seconds, you're kind of screwed.
>
> Finally, my last PIN was 8338... so what would I do in that circumstance??!

435.   Hand and finger scanners work the same way as you see in movies.

> There are many movies where a character needs to get through a locked door but it is sealed with a biometric scanner for scanning fingerprints. In some films, the character would chop off a security guard's hand and use it to gain clearance.
>
> However that doesn't work (and is disgusting.) Biometric scanners don't just scan your fingerprints. They scan your blood flow. Even iPhone's use this form of technology.

436.   Emptying your trashcan on your computer means your deleted files are gone forever.

> If your computer has a magnetic hard drive, (most of them do) the deleted file is probably sitting on your hard drive waiting to be overwritten. Nobody knows when the file will be overwritten so if you deleted something by accident, you can get it back but you will need to consult with an expert.

437.   Micro transactions are a recent video game development.

These are just as popular on iPhones games as they are on computer consoles.

What to get a secret character? Pay $5.

Want to skip to the next level of Candy Crush? Pay $1.99.

Can't play the rest of the game unless you pay? Pay $9.99.

Micro transactions seem like an infuriating recent addition to computer games but they have existed since 1990. In the arcade version of Double Dragon 3, you could access better weapons and characters if you put in more money.

438.   Video game players are predominantly male.

43% of video game players are female.

31% of video game players are female adults.

439.   The Nintendo Wii invented Motion-controlled computer consoles in 2006.

The Atari and Commodore consoles had motion-controlled sensors back in 1983. They used a stick called... Le Stick.

It didn't use light or weight sensors like the Wii or the Kinect. Instead it used motion detectors. Le Stick didn't do well because the sensors were powered by mercury. In case you don't know, mercury kind of gives you lethal diseases like ataxia and Minimata if it comes into contact with your skin.

440. Surgically inserting pacemakers involve a huge surgical procedure.

You would assume inserting a pacemaker into a person's heart would be a big deal. After all, it's the frickin' heart. As recently as 2007, pacemaker surgery required cutting into the chest and inserting a device the size of a 50-cent piece with 2 feet of trailing electrodes.

But nowadays, nano-pacemakers are used. They are ten times smaller and can be inserted through a vein.

UNSOLVED MYSTERIES

441. The Mary Celeste was a ship that was found empty. No one knows what happened to the crew.

The most famous "ghost ship" incident ever was the Mary Celeste. Even a skeptic would find this story scary.

In 1872, a ship was spotted in the Atlantic. There wasn't a single person onboard but everything seemed to be intact. There was no sign of a struggle or attack. Nothing seemed to be misplaced, not even valuables or piano music. There were no storms in the area and no money was stolen. Even their logbook was up to date. It was like the crew vanished into thin air.

But they didn't because that would be silly. What actually happened was way more stupid.

On further investigation, they did find something missing – nine barrels of alcohol. There was a leak in the barrels and once the vapor ignited (probably from wandering crew member's pipe) a pressure-wave explosion was created. This type of explosion is so bizarre that it would freak anyone out. The entire crew abandoned ship so suddenly that they took no supplies with them on their lifeboats. They all died of thirst days later.

Wait...hold on! How does anyone know this! There were no witnesses to confirm this so this is one heck of a farfetched theory.

But it has been tested. Chemistry teacher, Dr. Andrea Sella built a replica of the Mary Celeste in

2006. (Scientists have way too much time on their hands.) He ignited nine barrels of alcohol with a single spark creating a pressure explosion. This type of explosion is devastating but it wouldn't have caused any damage to the ship or the crew. But they didn't understand the science of it and assumed that their ship was haunted. I mean... wouldn't you?

442. Cow mutilations are a mystery.

Cows and sheep and other animals have been found with gaping holes in their bodies. But wild predators did not make these holes. The holes are perfectly circular as if a sci-fi laser caused them.

And if your rational mind is trying to comprehend this, there's one bigger factor – the animals are drained of their blood.

For the longest time, no one could think of a rational explanation as to why this happens. Then it was discovered that the explanation was simple and gross.

Maggots.

It turns out that predators like foxes DID cause the wounds.

The wounded animal would crawl off and die. When animals die, maggots feast on the dead flesh draining it of all blood. Maggots start eating at one point and then work their way around in a circular manner. This eventually creates a perfect circle.

For the longest time, conspiracy theorists blamed UFO's for these mutilations but it turns out the culprit was a lot closer to home.

443.   The Nazca people of Ancient Peru mysteriously vanished.

When an entire group of people mysteriously vanishes, it's always tempting to believe in some conspiracy theory but the fate of the Nazca people is tragically simple. They destroyed all of their trees to make room for their farming, having no idea that it would alter the climate. This prevented the growth of food and the entire Nazca population died out within a generation.

444.   Nothing can cure hiccups.

There are so many supposed ways to cure hiccups.

Holding your breath. Getting a sudden fright. Drinking a lot of water in one gulp. But nothing seems to work.

Except one thing.

A spoonful of sugar.

Seriously. All this time, Mary Poppins was right. This sounds like a primitive type of medicine that was used centuries ago. Surely there's a better cure nowadays.

But no. Dr. Edgar Engelman did a study in 1971 which can be viewed in the New England Hournal of Medicine which validates this theory. In his study, a spoonful of sugar worked 95% of the time. It even worked on patients who had hiccups for weeks.

The reason why is that the sudden sweetness overstimulates the vagus nerve (which connects your brain to the abdomen) which takes pressure off your diaphragm.

445. **Ball lightning are spheres of light that can pass through walls.**

Some speculation suggests that ball lightning is a UFO. And people who make such a speculation are commonly known as Completely Wrong.

Ball lightning occurs when lightning strikes land that is full of quartz or silica e.g. sand. The silica and electricity from the lightning form a vapor, which condenses into a ball of light when it has cooled.

Since it is light, this is why it passes through objects but since it has an electrical charge, this is why it has been known to burn things and even people.

446. **There are stones in Death Valley that move by themselves.**

Not only do the stones in Death Valley move, but they also suddenly change direction. These are not little stones. One of the "stones" was seven hundred pounds. Conspiracy theorists insist that aliens are behind it. In their defense, Area 51 is quite near.

But these stones move for a number of reasons. Death Valley has powerful winds, which are strong enough to move a big rock.

Even a seven hundred pound rock you may ask? Yes because the ground in Death Valley is slick and muddy.

Muddy? Slick? Isn't Death Valley a desert?

Usually. But every few years, a lake called Racetrack Playa floods, making all of the ground in the area slippery as well as shifting the rocks around. Some of the rocks are so heavy that they move in the water but they don't leave the ground. This makes the rock look like it's dragging itself. So some of the rocks move because of winds and some move because of water but none move for supernatural reasons.

<u>WAR</u>

447. Americans had the most casualties during World War II fighting the Nazis.
Less than 220,000 Americans died during WWII. Although Russians are seen as the enemy after the Second World War, 20 million of them died trying to stop the Nazis.

448. War deaths are rising.
Combat deaths are at their lowest in 100 years. According to data compiled by researchers at Peace Research Institute Oslo, the last decade had fewer deaths than any other decade in the past century.

449. During the American Civil War, the North was anti-racist.
History has simplified the American Civil War so the South appears to be made up of racist bigots and the North wanted to abolish slavery. It is true that the North had many passionate abolitionists.

But the black community was barred from many basic rights even after the abolition of slavery. Lynch mobs and riots were common in the North at the time. Also, the North had the most violent race riot in the history of America. The riots in the North got so dangerous that two years after slavery was abolished, the black community plunged to its lowest number in forty-five years.

450. **The American Civil War was the bloodiest war in American history.**

414,000 died during the Civil War but only 207,000 died in combat. Fewer than 300,000 American soldiers died in WWII. On top of that, another 625,000 American soldiers died in WWII from sickness or their injuries.

451. **There were no wars during the Cold War.**

There was no war between Russia and America during the Cold War, which lasted from 1945 to 1990 but the Korean, Vietnam and Afghanistan Wars were going on during that time.

452. **France suck at war.**

In all mediums, France is always satirized for surrendering in every battle.

However, France is a force to be reckoned with when it comes to battle. Out of the 168 major wars they have fought since 387 BC, they have won 109, drew in 10, and lost 49.

<u>WEAPONS</u>

453. The most powerful bomb detonation was in Hiroshima in World War II.
The most powerful bomb detonation was carried out by the Soviet Union in the Artic on October 30th, 1961. This twenty-seven ton Tsar Bomb was used to prove that the Soviets were a force to be reckoned with.

Upon detonation, it unleashed the force of 50 million tons of high explosive. That's 3,800 times more powerful than the bomb dropped on Hiroshima. The force shattered windows 600 miles away in Finland and the shockwave travelled around the Earth three times. Ironically, the Soviets could've made it twice as powerful but they thought that would be overkill. Because 50 million tons sounded perfectly reasonable to them for some reason.

454. Bomb detonators have visible digital timers.
This is a great way to build tension in a movie but bombs in real life don't have visible timers counting down.

455. Katanas are the greatest swords in the world.
This idea has been popularized thanks to many samurai movies (and Pulp Fiction.) There is no "best" sword. It depends on the craftsmanship. Nor is there any kind of indestructible sword. If a sword strikes a solid object a few dozen times, it will be rendered useless.

456.   Movies depict sword-making accurately.
The most iconic sword-forging scene in movie
history is from Conan the Barbarian (although
most films show the process the same way – you
heat the metal, bash it into a shape, and then heat
it again. Piece of cake.)

But forging swords isn't that easy. Making
one sword takes at least forty hours (but it can
take over three days.)

And that's just the blade. That's not including
the handle, the guard, or the pommel.

Even forging a single dagger can take up to
fifty hours.

Movies like Conan show swords starting off
as a boiling liquid. That technique hasn't been
used since the Bronze Age. (Who would ever have
thought a movie where the villain turns into a
snake would be inaccurate?)

Melting metal weakens its chemical bonds.
You need to always start with metal to forge a
sword nowadays.

457.   Snipers use lasers to aim at their targets.
Snipers are meant to be sneaky. Using lasers is
telling their targets that they are a targets,
depriving the snipers of their sneakiness. The
scope is all a professional sniper needs to shoot
his or her target.

458.   Flamethrowers are illegal in America.
They're not. Go nuts.

459. Flamethrowers are an unstoppable weapon.
No matter how cool you look wielding a
flamethrower, it's a completely impractical
weapon. It weights seventy pounds and it only
has ten seconds of usage.

460. Flesh wounds are harmless gunshot wounds.
Despite what Monty Python says in the movie,
The Holy Grail, flesh wounds are no laughing
matter. A study done on fifty-eight patients with
gunshot wounds to the shoulder found that four
months after the initial injury, fifty-one of them
were suffering from constant pain due to vascular
damage. Half of them ended up with partial or
complete loss of mobility in their arms.

**461. If you get shot, you will be fine once the bullet
is removed.**
Digging the bullet out of a gunshot wound is
unnecessary and dangerous. The heat from the
bullet sterilizes the wound, preventing the spread
of infection. Removing the bullet could sever
blood vessels. Some people have bullets still
inside them after years, sometimes even decades
as removing the bullet could kill them.

462. A car door will stop a bullet.
A lot of cops take cover behind car doors on
television and in movies but it's so ineffective at
stopping a bullet, it might as well be made of
cardboard.

463.   A gun can go off if dropped.

This famously happens in the film, True Lies. But gun regulations require extensive drop safety tests, to prevent this from happening. So True Lies was … a lie. But it's still awesome.

464.   You can aim two guns at once.

It looks really cool in True Lies (did True Lies invent every gun misconception?) but your eyes aren't designed to aim and fire at two targets simultaneously. Also, how would you reload?

465.   Soldiers run out of bullets often when using their guns.

In movies, people empty their clips at the most pivotal moment to build tension in the scene. But in reality, soldiers are constantly reloading their guns every opportunity they have. Why wouldn't they? It's a life or death situation! That's like not refueling your car until it runs out of gas!

466.   If you are a good shooter on the gun range, you will be a good shooter in combat.

There is little psychology when shooting on a gun range. There is ALWAYS psychology when shooting in combat since you can actually die. A study examined more than two hundred violent encounters and showed no connection between prowess on the gun range and combat effectiveness. A perfect marksman on the range can become a whimpering mess when he knows his life is in danger.

467. **Nail guns can be just as dangerous as guns.**
Nail guns are weapons of death in many movies –
Lethal Weapons 2, Final Destination 3, even Bond
nailed a guy (pun intended) in Casino Royale.
But nail guns have a safety mechanism so they
cant be fired unless they're pressed against a
hard, flat surface. They cannot be fired across a
room. If nail guns were as effective as they seem
in movies, they would replace guns as the most
effective weapon of choice.

468. **If you get shot, you are as good as dead.**
As long as your heart is still beating when you
arrive in a hospital, there is a 95% chance you
will survive a gunshot wound.

This is according to former chief medical
examiner, Dr. Vincent J. M. DiMaio, who is the
author of many books about gunshot wounds.

469. **You can suppress the sound of a gun firing**
with a cushion.
A gunshot is 165 decibels in volume.

To help you gauge how loud that is, a
motorcycle engine is 100 decibels. 120 decibels is
so loud that it is painful to the human ear. Once
you reach 140 decibels, you risk permanent
hearing damage.

This means you would suffer irreparable
damage if you were beside a gun being fired.

But if you fire a gun into a cushion, do you
know how loud it would be? 145 decibels… so

cushions do pretty much nothing to silence gunfire.

470. The most efficient way to tell if someone's fired a gun is to check for fingerprints.

At least 90% of fingerprints are wiped off a gun as soon as it's put in the person's pocket.

The best way to tell if a person has fired a gun is to detect if there's any powder residue on their clothing.

<u>WORDS</u>

471. **"Recur" and "reoccur" mean the same thing.**
"Recur" is something that happens over and over.
"Reoccur" is used to show that something has happened again.

472. **Cowboys called a cow-catching rope a "lasso."**
Mexicans called looped ropes "lassoes." Cowboys only ever called them ropes. How creative.

473. **"Cryogenics" means "to freeze people."**
"Cryogenics" is the study of what happens to things under extreme cold.
The study of freezing living things is called "cryonics."

474. **"Peruse" means to skim over or browse something.**
It has the opposite definition. It means "to read with thoroughness or care."

475. **"Nonplussed" means "unperturbed" or "unworried."**
It means the opposite. You feel nonplussed when you are utterly perplexed and confused.

476. **"Plethora" means "a vast amount."**
It means "too much of something."

477. Never begin a sentence with a conjunction like "but," "so," or "and."

The most common criticism I receive from my editor is "Stop starting sentences with 'but'!" According to the Chicago Manual of Style, there is no historical or grammatical foundation for not using "and" or "but" at the beginning of a sentence. In fact, as many as 10% of first-rate writing begins with conjunctions.

That shows what my editor knows! (But seriously, please keep editing my books.)

478. People overuse the word "literally" way too much nowadays.

When someone says, "I was so embarrassed, I literally died" it is clear the person should've used the word "figuratively" instead of "literally."

However this is not a recent concept.

In F. Scott Fitzgerald's novel, The Great Gatsby, the title character is described at one point as thus, "He literally glowed." Unless Gatsby is suffering from radiation poisoning, I believe Fitzgerald meant "figuratively." Many renowned writers like Mark Twain also used "literally" incorrectly.

So am I suggesting people nowadays are using it incorrectly? Not exactly. The word "literally" is used literally all of the time that it now has two definitions according to Webster's dictionary -

1. "in a literal sense or manner."
2. "For effect."

479. Paragraphs have a set number of sentences.
Your English teacher may have told you that a paragraph needs to have three to five sentences to justify a new paragraph.

But a new paragraph after one sentence is acceptable if the idea behind the sentence is clear.

Like this.

Or that.

Or even that.

This practice is becoming more common over the last few years to emphasize certain points, to build tension or to develop a character. The Oxford Guide to Plain English confirms this.

Trust me.

480. "Bemused" means "amused."
No. We already have a word for that known as "amused." Why would we make up another word that is spelt and pronounced almost the same? "Bemused" is defined as "a state of bewilderment and confusion."

481. Charles Dickens invented the word, "humbug" in his story, A Christmas Carol.
This word was used for over a century before this book was written.

482. "Pristine" means "spotless" or "as good as new."
Nope. It means "in the same state as it was originally in."

483. **You need to put an apostrophe in a possessive singular noun ending in the letter "s."**

If you don't know what that sentence above means... just skip to the next misconception.

If you think this misconception is too overly specific, it's rules like this that can make or break a new writer (I learned that the hard way.)

Let's look at an example.

Do you say "Jesus' disciples?"

Or do you say "Jesus's disciples?"

You'll be happy to know that there is no definitive correct way. Whichever way you choose, make sure to stick with it or it will come across as inconsistent.

484. **Don't split infinitives.**

An infinitive is a verb that begins with "to" like "to eat" or "to sleep."

Some say it is incorrect to split the infinitive. This means that you shouldn't put a word between "to" and the verb itself. So it is considered wrong to say "to quickly run" or "to peacefully sleep."

This is more of a rule of thumb rather than a rule set in stone. Some phrases simply sound better when you split the infinitive. Shakespeare did this all of the time. Probably the most famous split infinitive ever is the line from Star Trek, "To boldly go where no man has gone before." How rubbish would it sound if the line was "to go boldly where no man has gone before."

THE WORLD

485. **There are a couple of earthquakes per year.**
There are a million earthquakes every year.

Now you might assume that the majority of these quakes are so small that they can only be detected by scientific equipment. And that is true.

But up to 100,000 quakes can be felt by people each year. That's 275 earthquakes a day. These are still minor quakes. 100 potentially dangerous earthquakes occur each year but they are unnoticed because they often happen in uninhabited terrains like forests or deserts.

Each year, there are approximately 17 major earthquakes (7.0 on the Richter scale) and one great earthquake (8.0 or higher.)

486. **During a tornado storm, you should hide in a car.**
Tornados can lift cars off the ground and hurl them around. A strong tornado can crush a car completely. If you are in a car during a tornado storm, National Weather Service recommend that you get out of the car and run to safety, preferably to a house or basement.

487. **You should hide under a highway overpass during a tornado storm.**
This idea has become well known as survivors of storms have been found hiding under overpasses. However, research shows that in those cases, the

tornados didn't reach the highways. As stated before, the best solution is a house or basement.

488. You can tell how far away a storm is by counting the seconds between when you see lightning and when you hear thunder.

This idea became popularized by the movie, Poltergeist. The concept is accurate but the details are wrong.

If you see lightning and hear thunder ten seconds apart, most people believe that the storm is ten miles away. To calculate it correctly, you need to divide that number by five. So if you hear the thunder ten seconds after you see the lightning, it is only two miles away.

489. Sunflowers follow the sun.

This may sound absurd but sunflowers DO follow the sun but only when they are buds. As soon as the petals open, they face east. No one knows why.

490. The Ozone Layer is damaged irreparably.

Three hundred scientists have carried out studies that show the ozone layer will have recovered to its original state in forty years.

Ten Most Bizarre Misconceptions

491.   Animals that look similar are genetically linked.

A lot people find it hard to believe that apes are distant cousins of humans.

But we do have a lot of similarities to apes. However, there are many animals that are distant cousins to each other but bear almost no resemblance.

Hippos are related to dolphins.
Donkeys are related to rhinos.
Crabs are related to spiders.
I can do this all day.
And I just might.
Scorpions are related to ticks.
Jellyfish are related to coral.
Ants are related to bees.
Prawns are related to woodlice.

Everyone knows humans share a common ancestor with apes (unless you're in denial about the whole evolution thing) but did you know humans also share a relation with kangaroos! This was 70 million years ago but it is clear our ancestors were one and the same. Not only are some genes identical in kangaroos DNA to human DNA, but they are even sequenced in precisely the same order.

It works both ways. Some animals look identical but bare no genetic ancestry. Some fish have more genetic similarities to mammals than to each other.

492. Aristotle was a great philosopher.

Aristotle is the most famous philosopher of all time and is considered to be history's first scientist. His influence is unquestionable. He was one of the first to talk about physics, motion, causality, optics, particles, substance, understanding of memory, sleep, and dreams.

He also said that snot is part of your brain falling out of your nose...

He also believed that the brain was a cooling device and humans think with their hearts.

Ok, obviously this was thousands of years ago and all of the greatest minds said silly things.

But I have to make an exception of Aristotle because he believed in so many concepts that were absurd and even immoral.

He firmly believed that women were deformed men and they couldn't keep their emotions in check because their wombs wandered around their bodies. (A lot of his theories revolved around putting down women.)

He was adamant that slavery was necessary as some people were just designed to be slaves.

The most puzzling thing he believed was that flies have four legs. Every child knows that's wrong. What is weirder is that this misconception went unchallenged for centuries.

493. Same-sex marriages have only existed recently.

Same-sex marriage was normal until the 14th century before Byzantine Emperor Andronikos II Palaiologos outlawed it in 1302.

In the 19th century, a Nigerian woman called Ifeyinwa Olinke was married to nine wives. I am not singling out Ifeyinwa as if her circumstance is exceptional. It is just well documented and irrefutable. But there were many examples of same-sex marriages in Africa and they were very common in Sudan (especially among women.)

494.   You can make thousands of combinations with a deck of cards.

Every time you shuffle a deck of cards, you have made a combination nobody has ever made in history.

But how? How many combinations can there be? Millions? Billions? Trillions? Not even close. There are 80,658,175,170,943,878,571,660,636,856,403,766,975,289,505,440,883,277,824,000,000,000,000 combinations. That's seventy numbers. The actual word for this number is 80 vignitillion (which sounds like a Transformer.)

If you are wondering how this is possible, here's a simple way to understand it. There are 52 cards in a deck. There are 26 letters in the alphabet. How many different stories have been created from those 26 letters?

So if you ever feel like you haven't accomplished anything unique in your life, just shuffle a deck of cards and you have done something that has never happened ever.

Unless you don't know how to shuffle.
And I don't.

495.   Homer existed.

Homer is credited with writing The Iliad and The Odyssey. These two books are the backbone of all literature. Many wonderful stories and characters were created thanks to these epic tales.

Troy. Achilles. The Wooden Horse. The Greek War. The Cyclops. Battling sea monsters. Greek Gods involving themselves in human disputes. All credited to Homer.

Or maybe not.

It is possible that Homer existed but there is very little evidence to support it. The only thing that is supposedly known about him is that he was born blind. There is no record of his life, his family or even his surname. He may have shared these stories orally and other storytellers refined them over the decades or possibly centuries and made them what they are today. Some scholars and historians believe that "Homer" is simply a pseudonym for dozens of authors who wrote these Greek tales over the years.

496.   In America, you are considered an adult at twenty-one because that's when you become mature.

In America, you can legally drink at twenty-one. The reason that age was determined has nothing to do with maturity. Back in medieval times, twenty-one was the age where a man was strong enough to wear body armor.

Body armor is metal so it's very heavy. Any human of any size would struggle carrying armor. So when you reached an age where you could carry the armor, you were considered to be a man. Most men couldn't do this until they were at least twenty-one so that became the age where they were considered men.

Also, the legal age for drinking in Europe is eighteen (and therefore that's the age at which you are considered to be a man in Europe.) That's probably because Europe has been in WAY more wars than America and they needed a lot more soldiers.

497. **Herbal medicine has existed for 3,000 years.** 3,000 years sounds like a long time but herbal medicine is mind-bogglingly ancient. Herbal medicine goes back 50,000 years.

This is insane because homo sapiens (human beings) have only existed for approximately 60,000 years. But what is more bizarre is that our ancestors were not the first to use herbal medicine. Herbs were used by our distant cousins – the Neanderthals.

Now I don't want you to think that Neanderthals ate herbs because they were stupid enough to think that herbs were food. The chamomile and yarrow that they ate had no nutritional value and tasted awful.

Archeologists have found microscopic particles of these herbs in the skeletons of Neanderthals that lived long lives. These particular Neanderthals knew that the herbs were keeping them alive (or more specifically, creating anti-inflammatory agents.) It was like prehistoric ibuprofen.

498. When you are in a coma, you are unconscious for weeks or even months.

Television simplifies a coma like this – you are either unconscious and unaware of your surroundings or you're awake and you are aware of your surroundings.

But real comas are not that simple. When you are in a coma, you can speak to people, interact with people, recognize people and even walk around.

But because you are still in a "coma," you can get back into bed and fall into a deep unconsciousness and have no memory of any of the events you just experienced.

T.V. always depicts a comatose patient suddenly waking up with complete clarity. But the brain is so delicate that your body functions tend to return to you bit by bit. Doctors use the Glasgow Coma Scale to gauge coma progress from a score of three (deep unconsciousness) to fifteen, based on eye, verbal and motor responses.

499. The human body has 600 muscles.

This is a common misconception that most children have heard many times.

But the truth is very peculiar – we don't know how many muscles the human body has. Different experts give different answers.

There are three types of muscles – striated, (skeletal muscles that you can control) smooth (involuntarily controlled by nerves) and cardiac (pumping muscles like the heart.)

Striated muscle experts would say there are 650 muscles because that is how striated layers are connected to your bones.

But if you include all of your cardiac muscles, it's more like 850.

However, if you include your involuntary muscles, that number would be in the millions! The reason why that number is so high is because every hair on your body (not just those on your head) is attached to a teeny weeny muscle.

So there you go. Humanity can split an atom and go into space but we still can't decide how many muscles we have.

500. Gandhi was a saint.

Mahatma Gandhi has been synonymous with sainthood. He is often depicted as an incredibly moral man who would stop at nothing to live in a world where everyone is treated equally.

However, author, G.B. Singh gathered twenty years of Gandhi's notes, speeches and documents for his book, Gandhi: Behind the Mask of Divinity and has concluded that Gandhi was not what he seemed.

Gandhi passionately discriminated against Africans and called them "raw kaffirs." A "kaffir" is derogatory term than many Africans find the most insulting term that can be bestowed upon a human being.

This accusation of Gandhi is irrefutable because he wrote about his racism in sixteen columns in his own newspaper called Indian Opinion. Just to make sure everybody knew just how much he despised Africans, he wrote it in four languages.

But Africans were not the only people Gandhi detested. Gandhi told a biographer that during World War II, "the Jews should have willingly offered themselves to the butcher's knife."

He even gave up on his own people. During World War II, he said that India should be "left to anarchy."

He cheated on his wife countless times, prevented his children from being educated and would banish them from his home on a whim.

I could write twenty other horrible truths about the supposed saint but I will save you time – Gandhi was not a nice man.

I hate to end the book on such a downer but it's not just the misconception itself that is significant but how it was discovered. The book's author, Singh is not just a researcher of Gandhi; he was a follower of Gandhi's teachings.

So why did Singh turn against the man he admired? The answer is simple – to learn.

If you were Christian, you would naturally dismiss any information that looks at Christianity in a negative light.

If you don't believe in evolution, you would dismiss any argument that strengthens the argument for evolution.

But Singh didn't think like this. He followed Gandhi's teachings for years until he read an article dismissing him in 1983. Singh didn't believe the article was true at first but he wanted to give it the benefit of a doubt. If he was going to follow the teachings of Gandhi, he had to make sure there was no doubt that Gandhi was as pure as he claimed to be. He believed that you cannot follow any ideal blindly, even if the idea has nothing but good intentions. It turned out that the article was right and Singh's life changed forever.

Isn't that amazing? We all want to protect our beliefs and we can become defensive and offensive when they are questioned. But Singh didn't care about being right. He just wanted to know the truth.

I can't think of any example that shows why I wrote these books. If you question any of these facts, don't dismiss them. Research them. You might be right but you might be wrong.

I might be wrong. And if I am wrong, then I will correct them. Any beliefs I have, no matter how strong they are, can change if I find alternative evidence. And I believe we should all live the same way.

Thanks for reading

34380644R00093

Made in the USA
San Bernardino, CA
26 May 2016